Cram101 Textbook Outlines to accompany:

Strategic Management of Technology and Innovation

Robert A. Burgelman, 5th Edition

A Content Technologies Inc. publication (c) 2011.

Learning System

Cram101 Textbook Outlines is a learning system. The notes in this book are the highlights of your textbook, you will never have to highlight a book again.

How to use this book. Take this book to class, it is your notebook for the lecture. The notes and highlights on the left hand side of the pages follow the outline and order of the textbook. All you have to do is follow along while your instructor presents the lecture. Circle the items emphasized in class and add other important information on the right side. With Cram101 Textbook Outlines you'll spend less time writing and more time listening. Learning becomes more efficient.

Cram101.com Online

Increase your studying efficiency by using Cram101.com's practice tests and online reference material. It is the perfect complement to Cram101 Textbook Outlines. Use self-teaching matching tests or simulate in-class testing with comprehensive multiple choice tests, or simply use Cram's true and false tests for quick review. Cram101.com even allows you to enter your in-class notes for an integrated studying format combining the textbook notes with your class notes.

Visit **www.Cram101.com**, click Sign Up at the top of the screen, and enter **DK73DW11677** in the promo code box on the registration screen. Your access to www.Cram101.com is discounted by 50% because you have purchased this book. Sign up and stop highlighting textbooks forever.

 ISBN(s): 1428884033. PUBI-2.2010128

Strategic Management of Technology and Innovation
Robert A. Burgelman, 5th

CONTENTS

1. TECHNOLOGICAL INNOVATION 2
2. TECHNOLOGICAL INNOVATION AND STRATEGY 24
3. TECHNOLOGICAL EVOLUTION 58
4. INDUSTRY CONTEXT 80
5. STRATEGIC ACTION 110
6. INTERNAL AND EXTERNAL SOURCES OF TECHNOLOGY 134
7. LINKING NEW TECHNOLOGY AND NOVEL CUSTOMER NEEDS 148
8. INTERNAL CORPORATE VENTURING 174
9. NEW PRODUCT DEVELOPMENT 196
10. BUILDING COMPETENCE/CAPABILITIES THROUGH NEW PRODUCT DEVELOPMENT 216

Chapter 1. TECHNOLOGICAL INNOVATION

Nominative determinism	Nominative determinism refers to the theory that a person`s name is given an influential role in reflecting key attributes of his job, profession, but real examples are more highly prized, the more obscure the better.
Group	In business, a group, business group, corporate group) alliance is most commonly a legal entity that is a type of conglomerate or holding company consisting of a parent company and subsidiaries. Typical examples are Adidas group or Icelandair group. In United Arab Emirates, Business group can also be knows as Trade association.
Case study	A Case study is one of several ways of doing research whether it is social science related or even socially related. It is an intensive study of a single group, incident, or community. Other ways include experiments, surveys, or analysis of archival information.
Market	A Market is any one of a variety of different systems, institutions, procedures, social relations and infrastructures whereby persons trade, and goods and services are exchanged, forming part of the economy. It is an arrangement that allows buyers and sellers to exchange things. Markets vary in size, range, geographic scale, location, types and variety of human communities, as well as the types of goods and services traded.
Mechanism	In philosophy, mechanism is the theory that all natural phenomena can be explained by laws of nature. It`s the opposite of vitalism, which claims organisms have `vital forces` which aren`t physical. The doctrine of mechanism in philosophy comes in two different flavors.
Volkswagen	The Volkswagen Automobile Company is an automobile manufacturer based in Wolfsburg, Germany, and is the original brand within the Volkswagen Group, as well as the largest brand by sales volume. Volkswagen means `people`s car` in German, in which it is pronounced . Its current tagline or slogan is Das Auto .
Volvo	The Volvo Group is a Swedish supplier of commercial vehicles such as trucks, buses and construction equipment, drive systems for marine and industrial applications, aerospace components and financial services. Although Volvo was incorporated in 1915 as a subsidiary of AB SKF, a Swedish ball bearing manufacturer, the auto manufacturer was officially founded on 14 April 1927, when the first car rolled out of the factory in Hisingen, Gothenburg. Volvo means `I roll` in Latin, conjugated from `volvere` .
Barriers to entry	In economics and mostly especially in the theory of competition, Barriers to entry are obstacles in the path of a firm that make it difficult to enter a given market.

	Barriers to entry protect incumbant firms from competition from newcomers. Barriers to entry are the source of a firm`s pricing power - the ability of a firm to raise prices without losing all its customers.
Communications management	Communications management is the systematic planning, implementing, monitoring, and revision of all the channels of communication within an organization, and between organizations; it also includes the organization and dissemination of new communication directives connected with an organization, network, designing internal and external communications directives, and managing the flow of information, including online communication. New technology forces constant innovation on the part of communications managers.
Economic profit	In neoclassical economics, economic profit is the difference between a firm`s total revenue and its opportunity costs. In classical economics profit is the return to the employer of capital stock in any productive pursuit involving labor. These two definitions are actually the same.
Innovation	Innovation is a change in the thought process for doing something or `new stuff that is made useful`. It may refer to an incremental emergent or radical and revolutionary changes in thinking, products, processes, or organizations. Following Schumpeter (1934), contributors to the scholarly literature on Innovation typically distinguish between invention, an idea made manifest, and Innovation, ideas applied successfully in practice.
Difference in differences	Difference in differences is a nonexperimental technique used in econometrics that measures the effect of a treatment at a given period in time. It is often used to measure the change induced by a particular treatment or event, though may be subject to certain biases (mean reversion bias, etc) The basic premise of `diff-in-diffs` is to examine the effect of some sort of treatment by comparing the treatment group after treatment both to the treatment group before treatment and to some other control group. Naively, you might consider simply looking at the treatment group before and after treatment to try to deduce the effect of the treatment.

Chapter 1. TECHNOLOGICAL INNOVATION

Intellectual property	Intellectual property is a term referring to a number of distinct types of creations of the mind for which property rights are recognised--and the corresponding fields of law. Under Intellectual property law, owners are granted certain exclusive rights to a variety of intangible assets, such as musical, literary, and artistic works; discoveries and inventions; and words, phrases, symbols, and designs. Common types of Intellectual property include copyrights, trademarks, patents, industrial design rights and trade secrets in some jurisdictions.
Xerox	Xerox Corporation is a global document management company which manufactures and sells a range of color and black-and-white printers, multifunction systems, photo copiers, digital production printing presses, and related consulting services and supplies. Xerox is headquartered in Norwalk, Connecticut , though its largest population of employees is based in and around Rochester, New York, the area in which the company was founded. The Xerox 914 was the first one-piece plain paper photocopier, and sold in the thousands. Xerox was founded in 1906 in Rochester, New York as `The Haloid Company`, which originally manufactured photographic paper and equipment.
Limitations	Limitations is a novel by Scott Turow which was published in 2006. It is by far his shortest novel (197 pages) and prior to publication as a novel was released as a serial story in the Sunday New York Times Magazine. As Turow`s other novels, it is set in fictional Kindle County in Illinois, and he revives some familiar characters, including George Mason from Personal Injuries and Rusty Sabich, the hero of his acclaimed fiction debut, Presumed Innocent. Mason is now a judge, faced with the challenge of deciding a high-profile case involving a rape case that reawakens his long-suppressed guilt over his own role in a similar incident decades before.
Dominant design	Dominant Design is a Technology Management concept identifying key technological designs that become a de-facto standard in their market place. When a new technology emerges (e.g. computer GUI operating systems) - often firms will introduce a number of alternative designs (e.g. Microsoft - Windows, Apple Inc. - Mac OS and IBM - OS2) .
Tacit knowledge	Tacit knowledge is knowledge that is difficult to transfer to another person by means of writing it down or verbalising it. For example, stating to someone that Tooting is in London is a piece of explicit knowledge that can be written down, transmitted, and understood by a recipient. However the ability to speak a language, use algebra, or design and use complex equipment requires all sorts of knowledge that is not always known explicitly, even by expert practitioners, and which is difficult to explicitly transfer to users.

Trade secret

A Trade secret is a formula, practice, process, design, instrument, pattern, or compilation of information which is not generally known or reasonably ascertainable, by which a business can obtain an economic advantage over competitors or customers. In some jurisdictions, such secrets are referred to as `confidential information` or `classified information`.

The precise language by which a Trade secret is defined varies by jurisdiction . However, there are three factors that, although subject to differing interpretations, are common to all such definitions: a Trade secret is information that:

· is not generally known to the public;

· confers some sort of economic benefit on its holder (where this benefit must derive specifically from its not being generally known, not just from the value of the information itself);

· is the subject of reasonable efforts to maintain its secrecy

By comparison, under US law, `A Trade secret, as defined under 18 U.S.C. Â§ 1839(3) (A), (B) (1996), has three parts: (1) information; (2) reasonable measures taken to protect the information; and (3) which derives independent economic value from not being publicly known.`

A company can protect its confidential information through non-compete and non-disclosure contracts with its employees (within the constraints of employment law, including only restraint that is reasonable in geographic and time scope).

Complementary assets

Complementary assets are assets, infrastructure or capabilities needed to support the successful commercialization and marketing of a technological innovation, other than those assets fundamentally associated with that innovation. The term was first coined by David Teece. Key empirical studies on Complementary assets were conducted by Frank T. Rothaermel. Complementary assets are broken down into three general types:

· Generic assets: `general purpose` assets which do not need to be tailored to a particular innovation;

	· Specialized assets: unilateral dependence between the innovation and the complementary asset; · Cospecialized assets: bilateral dependence between the innovation and the complementary asset.
Niche market	A Niche market is the subset of the market on which a specific product is focusing; therefore the market niche defines the specific product features aimed at satisfying specific market needs, as well as the price range, production quality and the demographics that is intended to impact. Every single product that is on sale can be defined by its Niche market. As of special note, the products aimed at a wide demographic audience, with the resulting low price , are said to belong to the mainstream niche--in practice referred to only as mainstream or of high demand.
Asset	In financial accounting, Assets are economic resources. Anything tangible or intangible that is capable of being owned or controlled to produce value and that is held to have positive economic value is considered an Asset. Simplistically stated, Assets represent ownership of value that can be converted into cash (although cash itself is also considered an Asset).
Single version of the truth	In computerized business management, Single version of the truth is a technical concept describing the data warehousing ideal of having either a single centralised database, or at least a distributed synchronised database, which stores all of an organisation`s data in a consistent and non-redundant form. In some systems and in the context of message processing systems (often realtime systems), this term also refers to the goal of establishing a single agreed sequence of messages within a database formed by a particular but arbitrary sequencing of records. The key concept is that data combined in a certain sequence is a `truth` which may be analyzed and processed giving particular results, and that although the sequence is arbitrary (and thus another correct but equally arbitrary sequencing would ultimately provide different results in any analysis), it is desirable to agree that the sequence enshrined in the `Single version of the truth` is the version that will be considered `the truth`, and that any conclusions drawn from analysis of the database are valid and unarguable, and (in a technical context) the database may be duplicated to a backup environment to ensure a persistent record is kept of the `Single version of the truth`.

Chapter 1. TECHNOLOGICAL INNOVATION

Hostile work environment	A Hostile work environment exists when an employee experiences workplace harassment and fears going to work because of the offensive, intimidating, religion, sex, national origin, age, disability, veteran status, or, in some jurisdictions, sexual orientation, political affiliation, citizenship status, marital status, or personal appearance. Hostile work environment is also one of the two legal categories of sexual harassment. A Hostile work environment may also be defined as when a boss or manager begins to engage in a manner designed to make you quit in retaliation for your actions.
Vertical integration	In microeconomics and management, the term Vertical integration describes a style of management control. Vertically integrated companies in a supply chain are united through a common owner. Usually each member of the supply chain produces a different product or (market-specific) service, and the products combine to satisfy a common need.
Regulations	The Control of Substances Hazardous to Health regulations 2002 is a United Kingdom Statutory Instrument that stipulates general requirements on employers to protect employees and other persons from the hazards of substances used at work by risk assessment, control of exposure, health surveillance and incident planning. There are also duties on employees to take care of their own exposure to hazardous substances and prohibitions on the import of certain substances into the European Economic Area. The regulations reenacted with amendements the Control of Substances Hazardous to Work regulations 1999 and implement several European Union directives.
Equal	EQUAL was the `Community Initiative` within the European Social Fund of the European Union. It concerned `transnational co-operation to promote new means of combating all forms of discrimination and inEQUALities in connection with the labour market`. It ran from 2001 till 2007 with a budget of some â,¬3 billion of EU resources, matched by a similar sum from national resources.
Trademark	A Trademark is a distinctive sign or indicator used by an individual, business organization, or other legal entity to identify that the products and/or services to consumers with which the Trademark appears originate from a unique source and to distinguish its products or services from those of other entities.
Research and development	The phrase Research and development according to the Organization for Economic Co-operation and Development, refers to `creative work undertaken on a systematic basis in order to increase the stock of knowledge, including knowledge of man, culture and society, and the use of this stock of knowledge to devise new applications`.

New product design and development is more often than not a crucial factor in the survival of a company. In an industry that is fast changing, firms must continually revise their design and range of products.

Market dominance

Market dominance is a measure of the strength of a brand, product, service, relative to competitive offerings. There is often a geographic element to the competitive landscape. In defining Market dominance, you must see to what extent a product, brand, or firm controls a product category in a given geographic area.

Competitiveness

Competitiveness is a comparative concept of the ability and performance of a firm, sub-sector or country to sell and supply goods and/or services in a given market. Although widely used in economics and business management, the usefulness of the concept, particularly in the context of national competitiveness, is vigorously disputed by economists, such as Paul Krugman .

The term may also be applied to markets, where it is used to refer to the extent to which the market structure may be regarded as perfectly competitive.

Trade barrier

A Trade barrier is a general term that describes any government policy or regulation that restricts international trade. The barriers can take many forms, including the following terms that include many restrictions in international trade within multiple countries that import and export any items of trade.

· Import duty
· Import licenses
· Export licenses
· Import quotas
· Tariffs
· Subsidies
· Non-tariff barriers to trade
· Voluntary Export Restraints
· Local Content Requirements
· Embargo

Most trade barriers work on the same principle: the imposition of some sort of cost on trade that raises the price of the traded products. If two or more nations repeatedly use trade barriers against each other, then a trade war results.

Trade barriers

Trade barriers are a general term that describes any government policy or regulation that restricts international trade. The barriers can take many forms, including the following terms that include many restrictions in international trade within multiple countries that import and export any items of trade:

· Tariffs

· Import licenses

· Export licenses

· Import quotas

· Subsidies

· Non-tariff barriers to trade

· Voluntary Export Restraints

· Local Content Requirements

· Embargo

Most Trade barriers work on the same principle: the imposition of some sort of cost on trade that raises the price of the traded products. If two or more nations repeatedly use Trade barriers against each other, then a trade war results.

Economists generally agree that Trade barriers are detrimental and decrease overall economic efficiency, this can be explained by the theory of comparative advantage.

Market research

Market research is any organized effort to gather information about markets or customers. It is a very important component of business strategy. The term is commonly interchanged with marketing research; however, expert practitioners may wish to draw a distinction, in that marketing research is concerned specifically about marketing processes, while Market research is concerned specifically with markets.

Chapter 1. TECHNOLOGICAL INNOVATION

Planning	Planning in organizations and public policy is both the organizational process of creating and maintaining a plan; and the psychological process of thinking about the activities required to create a desired goal on some scale. As such, it is a fundamental property of intelligent behavior. This thought process is essential to the creation and refinement of a plan, or integration of it with other plans, that is, it combines forecasting of developments with the preparation of scenarios of how to react to them.
Strategic planning	Strategic planning is an organization`s process of defining its strategy, or direction, and making decisions on allocating its resources to pursue this strategy, including its capital and people. Various business analysis techniques can be used in Strategic planning, including SWOT analysis (Strengths, Weaknesses, Opportunities, and Threats), PEST analysis (Political, Economic, Social, and Technological), STEER analysis (Socio-cultural, Technological, Economic, Ecological, and Regulatory factors), and EPISTEL . Strategic planning is the formal consideration of an organization`s future course. All Strategic planning deals with at least one of three key questions:  · `What do we do?`  · `For whom do we do it?`  · `How do we excel?` In business Strategic planning, the third question is better phrased `How can we beat or avoid competition?`.
Demand	In economics, Demand is the desire to own anything and the ability to pay for it and willigness to pay . The term Demand signifies the ability or the willingness to buy a particular commodity at a given point of time. Demand is also defined elsewhere as a measure of preferences that is weighted by income.
Operating cost	Operating costs are the recurring expenses which are related to the operation of a business, or to the operation of a device, component, piece of equipment or facility. For a commercial enterprise, Operating costs fall into two broad categories: · fixed costs, which are the same whether the operation is closed or running at 100% capacity

· variable costs, which may increase depending on whether more production is done, and how it is done.

Competitive advantage

Competitive advantage is a position of a company in a competitive landscape that allows the company earning return on investments higher than the cost of investments. Competitive advantage should be relevant, unique, and sustainable.

Competitive advantage is a theory that seeks to address some of the criticisms of comparative advantage.

Core competency

A Core competency is a specific factor that a business sees as being central to the way it, or its employees, works. It fulfills three key criteria:

· It provides consumer benefits

· It is not easy for competitors to imitate

· It can be leveraged widely to many products and markets
A Core competency can take various forms, including technical/subject matter know-how, a reliable process and/or close relationships with customers and suppliers. It may also include product development or culture, such as employee dedication.

Core competencies are particular strengths relative to other organizations in the industry which provide the fundamental basis for the provision of added value.

Decentralization

Delegation is a more extensive form of Decentralization. Through delegation central governments transfer responsibility for decision-making and administration of public functions to semi-autonomous organizations not wholly controlled by the central government, but ultimately accountable to it. Governments delegate responsibilities when they create public enterprises or corporations, housing authorities, transportation authorities, special service districts, semi-autonomous school districts, regional development corporations, or special project implementation units.

Strategic business unit	Strategic business unit is understood as a business unit within the overall corporate identity which is distinguishable from other business because it serves a defined external market where management can conduct strategic planning in relation to products and markets. The unique small business unit benefits that a firm aggressively promotes in a consistent manner. When companies become really large, they are best thought of as being composed of a number of businesses (or Strategic business units).
Outsourcing	Outsourcing often refers to the process of contracting to a third-party. While Outsourcing may be viewed as a component to the growing division of labor encompassing all societies, the term did not enter the English-speaking lexicon until the 1980s. Since the 1980s, transnational corporations have increased subcontracting across national boundaries.
Gold Star	The Gold Star medal is a special insignia that identifies recipients of the title \`Hero\` in the Soviet Union and several post-Soviet states. The Gold Star was established by the decree of the Presidium of the Supreme Soviet on August 1, 1939. Previously, Heroes of the Soviet Union were awarded the Order of Lenin and a special diploma (gramota, Ð³Ñ€Ð°Ð¼Ð¾Ñ,Ð°) describing the heroic feat. The medal was introduced to distinguish these heroes from other Order of Lenin recipients.
Career	Career is a term defined by the Oxford English Dictionary as an individual\`s \`course or progress through life \`. It is usually considered to pertain to remunerative work (and sometimes also formal education). The etymology of the term is somewhat ironic in that it comes from the Latin word carrera, which means race .
Enterprise resource planning	Enterprise resource planning is an Integrated computer-based system used to manage internal and external resources, including tangible assets, financial resources, materials, and human resources. It is a software architecture whose purpose is to facilitate the flow of information between all business functions inside the boundaries of the organization and manage the connections to outside stakeholders. Built on a centralized database and normally utilizing a common computing platform, Enterprise resource planning systems consolidate all business operations into a uniform and enterprise-wide system environment.

Chapter 2. TECHNOLOGICAL INNOVATION AND STRATEGY

Case study	A Case study is one of several ways of doing research whether it is social science related or even socially related. It is an intensive study of a single group, incident, or community. Other ways include experiments, surveys, or analysis of archival information.
Camera	A Camera is a device that records images, either as a still photograph or as moving images known as videos or movies. The term comes from the Camera obscura , an early mechanism of projecting images where an entire room functioned as a real-time imaging system; the modern Camera evolved from the Camera obscura. Cameras may work with the light of the visible spectrum or with other portions of the electromagnetic spectrum.
Venture capital	Venture capital is provided as seed funding to early-stage, high-potential, growth companies and more often after the seed funding round as growth funding round (also referred as series A round) in the interest of generating a return through an eventual realization event such as an IPO or trade sale of the company. To put it simply, an investment firm will give money to a growing company. The growing company will then use this money to advertise, do research, build infrastructure, develop products etc.
Advanced Micro Devices	Advanced Micro Devices, Inc. is an American multinational semiconductor company based in Sunnyvale, California, that develops computer processors and related technologies for commercial and consumer markets. Its main products include microprocessors, motherboard chipsets, embedded processors and graphics processors for servers, workstations and personal computers, and processor technologies for handheld devices, digital television, automobiles, game consoles, and other embedded systems applications.
Innovation	Innovation is a change in the thought process for doing something or `new stuff that is made useful`. It may refer to an incremental emergent or radical and revolutionary changes in thinking, products, processes, or organizations. Following Schumpeter (1934), contributors to the scholarly literature on Innovation typically distinguish between invention, an idea made manifest, and Innovation, ideas applied successfully in practice.
Business plan	A Business plan is a formal statement of a set of business goals, the reasons why they are believed attainable, and the plan for reaching those goals. It may also contain background information about the organization or team attempting to reach those goals.
Constraint	In mathematics, a constraint is a condition that a solution to an optimization problem must satisfy. There are two types of constraints: equality constraints and inequality constraints. The set of solutions that satisfy all constraints is called the feasible set.

Business process	A Business process or business method is a collection of related, structured activities or tasks that produce a specific service or product for a particular customer or customers. It often can be visualized with a flowchart as a sequence of activities. Overview There are three types of Business processes: · Management processes, the processes that govern the operation of a system. Typical management processes include `Corporate Governance` and `Strategic Management`. · Operational processes, processes that constitute the core business and create the primary value stream. Typical operational processes are Purchasing, Manufacturing, Marketing and Sales. · Supporting processes, which support the core processes. Examples include Accounting, Recruitment, Technical support.
Copyright	Copyright is the set of exclusive rights granted to the author or creator of an original work, including the right to copy, distribute and adapt the work. These rights can be licensed, transferred and/or assigned. Copyright lasts for a certain time period after which the work is said to enter the public domain.
Market dominance	Market dominance is a measure of the strength of a brand, product, service, relative to competitive offerings. There is often a geographic element to the competitive landscape. In defining Market dominance, you must see to what extent a product, brand, or firm controls a product category in a given geographic area.
Market	A Market is any one of a variety of different systems, institutions, procedures, social relations and infrastructures whereby persons trade, and goods and services are exchanged, forming part of the economy. It is an arrangement that allows buyers and sellers to exchange things. Markets vary in size, range, geographic scale, location, types and variety of human communities, as well as the types of goods and services traded.
Emission standards	Emission standards are requirements that set specific limits to the amount of pollutants that can be released into the environment. Many emissions standards focus on regulating pollutants released by automobiles and other powered vehicles but they can also regulate emissions from industry, power plants, small equipment such as lawn mowers and diesel generators. Frequent policy alternatives to emissions standards are technology standards or soot, carbon monoxide (CO), or volatile hydrocarbons .

Hostile work environment	A Hostile work environment exists when an employee experiences workplace harassment and fears going to work because of the offensive, intimidating, religion, sex, national origin, age, disability, veteran status, or, in some jurisdictions, sexual orientation, political affiliation, citizenship status, marital status, or personal appearance. Hostile work environment is also one of the two legal categories of sexual harassment. A Hostile work environment may also be defined as when a boss or manager begins to engage in a manner designed to make you quit in retaliation for your actions.
Asset	In financial accounting, Assets are economic resources. Anything tangible or intangible that is capable of being owned or controlled to produce value and that is held to have positive economic value is considered an Asset. Simplistically stated, Assets represent ownership of value that can be converted into cash (although cash itself is also considered an Asset).
Complementary assets	Complementary assets are assets, infrastructure or capabilities needed to support the successful commercialization and marketing of a technological innovation, other than those assets fundamentally associated with that innovation. The term was first coined by David Teece. Key empirical studies on Complementary assets were conducted by Frank T. Rothaermel. Complementary assets are broken down into three general types: · Generic assets: \`general purpose\` assets which do not need to be tailored to a particular innovation; · Specialized assets: unilateral dependence between the innovation and the complementary asset; · Cospecialized assets: bilateral dependence between the innovation and the complementary asset.
Modularity	Modularity is a general systems concept, typically defined as a continuum describing the degree to which a system\`s components may be separated and recombined. It refers to both the tightness of coupling between components, and the degree to which the \`rules\` of the system architecture enable the mixing and matching of components.

Lawrence Livermore National Laboratory	The Lawrence Livermore National Laboratory in Livermore, California is a scientific research laboratory founded by the University of California in 1952. It is primarily funded by the United States Department of Energy (DOE) and managed and operated by Lawrence Livermore National Security, LLC (LLNS), a partnership of the University of California, Bechtel Corporation, Babcock and Wilcox, the URS Corporation, and Battelle Memorial Institute. On October 1, 2007 LLNS assumed management of Lawrence Livermore National Laboratory from the University of California, which had exclusively managed and operated the Laboratory since its inception 55 years before. Lawrence Livermore National Laboratory is self-described as `a premier research and development institution for science and technology applied to national security.` Its principal responsibility is ensuring the safety, security and reliability of the nation`s nuclear weapons through the application of advanced science, engineering and technology.
Transmeta	Transmeta Corporation was a US-based corporation that licensed low power semiconductor intellectual property. Transmeta originally produced very long instruction word code morphing (microcoded) microprocessors, with a focus on reducing power consumption in electronic devices. It was founded in 1995 by Bob Cmelik, Dave Ditzel , Colin Hunter, Ed Kelly, Doug Laird, Malcolm Wing, and Greg Zyner.
Team	A team comprises a group of people or animals linked in a common purpose. teams are especially appropriate for conducting tasks that are high in complexity and have many interdependent subtasks. A group in itself does not necessarily constitute a team.
Intellectual property	Intellectual property is a term referring to a number of distinct types of creations of the mind for which property rights are recognised--and the corresponding fields of law. Under Intellectual property law, owners are granted certain exclusive rights to a variety of intangible assets, such as musical, literary, and artistic works; discoveries and inventions; and words, phrases, symbols, and designs. Common types of Intellectual property include copyrights, trademarks, patents, industrial design rights and trade secrets in some jurisdictions.
Plants	Plants are living organisms belonging to the kingdom Plantae. They include familiar organisms such as trees, herbs, bushes, grasses, vines, ferns, mosses, and green algae. The scientific study of plants, known as botany, has identified about 350,000 extant species of plants, defined as seed plants, bryophytes, ferns and fern allies.

Card check	Card check is a method for American employees to organize into a labor union in which a majority of employees in a bargaining unit sign authorization forms,` stating they wish to be represented by the union. Since the National Labor Relations Act (NLRA) became law in 1935, majority sign-up has been an alternative to the National Labor Relations Board`s (NLRB) election process. There are two main differences between majority sign-up and the NLRB election process.
Group	In business, a group, business group, corporate group) alliance is most commonly a legal entity that is a type of conglomerate or holding company consisting of a parent company and subsidiaries. Typical examples are Adidas group or Icelandair group. In United Arab Emirates, Business group can also be knows as Trade association.
Multiple correspondence analysis	In statistics, Multiple correspondence analysis is a data analysis technique for nominal or categorical data, used to detect and represent underlying structures in a data set. It does this by representing individuals as points in a low-dimensional Euclidean space. The procedure thus appears to be the counterpart of principal component analysis for categorical data.
Business model	A Business model describes the rationale of how an organization creates, delivers, and captures value - economic, social, or other forms of value. The process of Business model design is part of business strategy. In theory and practice the term Business model is used for a broad range of informal and formal descriptions to represent core aspects of a business, including purpose, offerings, strategies, infrastructure, organizational structures, trading practices, and operational processes and policies.
Business-to-business	Business-to-business describes commerce transactions between businesses, such as between a manufacturer and a wholesaler, or between a wholesaler and a retailer. Contrasting terms are business-to-consumer (B2C) and business-to-government (B2G). The volume of B2B transactions is much higher than the volume of B2C transactions.
Business-to-consumer	Business-to-consumer describes activities of businesses serving end consumers with products and/or services.

An example of a B2C transaction would be a person buying a pair of shoes from a retailer. The transactions that led to the shoes being available for purchase, that is the purchase of the leather, laces, rubber, etc.

First-mover advantage	First-mover advantage is the advantage gained by the initial occupant of a market segment. This advantage may stem from the fact that the first entrant can gain control of resources that followers may not be able to match. Sometimes the first mover is not able to capitalise on its advantage, leaving the opportunity for another firm to gain second-mover advantage.
Regulations	The Control of Substances Hazardous to Health regulations 2002 is a United Kingdom Statutory Instrument that stipulates general requirements on employers to protect employees and other persons from the hazards of substances used at work by risk assessment, control of exposure, health surveillance and incident planning. There are also duties on employees to take care of their own exposure to hazardous substances and prohibitions on the import of certain substances into the European Economic Area. The regulations reenacted with amendements the Control of Substances Hazardous to Work regulations 1999 and implement several European Union directives.
Target market	A Target market is a group of customers that the business has decided to aim its marketing efforts and ultimately its merchandise. A well-defined Target market is the first element to a marketing strategy. The Target market and the marketing mix variables of product, place (distribution), promotion and price are the two elements of a marketing mix strategy that determine the success of a product in the marketplace.
Basic indicator approach	Basic indicator approach is a set of operational risk measurement techniques proposed under Basel II capital adequacy rules for banking institutions. Basel II requires all banking institutions to set aside capital for operational risk. Basic indicator approach is much simpler compared to the alternative approaches (i.e. standardized approach (operational risk) and advanced measurement approach) and this has been recommended for banks without significant international operations.
Generalized additive model	In statistics, the Generalized additive model is a statistical model developed by Trevor Hastie and Rob Tibshirani for blending properties of generalized linear models with additive models.

The model specifies a distribution (such as a normal distribution, or a binomial distribution) and a link function g relating the expected value of the distribution to the predictors, and attempts to fit functions f_i to satisfy:

$$g(\mathrm{E}(Y)) = \beta_0 + f_1(x_1) + f_2(x_2) + \cdots + f_m(x_m).$$

The functions $f_i(x_i)$ may be fit using parametric or non-parametric means, thus providing the potential for better fits to data than other methods. The method hence is very general - a typical Generalized additive model might use a scatterplot smoothing function such as a locally weighted mean for $f_1(x_1)$, and then use a factor model for $f_2(x_2)$. By allowing nonparametric fits, well designed Generalized additive models allow good fits to the training data with relaxed assumptions on the actual relationship, perhaps at the expense of interpretability of results.

Nominative determinism

Nominative determinism refers to the theory that a person`s name is given an influential role in reflecting key attributes of his job, profession, but real examples are more highly prized, the more obscure the better.

Activity-based costing

Activity-based costing is a costing model that identifies activities in an organization and assigns the cost of each activity resource to all products and services according to the actual consumption by each: it assigns more indirect costs (overhead) into direct costs.

In this way an organization can precisely estimate the cost of its individual products and services for the purposes of identifying and eliminating those which are unprofitable and lowering the prices of those which are overpriced.

In a business organization, the Activity based costing methodology assigns an organization`s resource costs through activities to the products and services provided to its customers.

Strategic planning

Strategic planning is an organization`s process of defining its strategy, or direction, and making decisions on allocating its resources to pursue this strategy, including its capital and people. Various business analysis techniques can be used in Strategic planning, including SWOT analysis (Strengths, Weaknesses, Opportunities, and Threats), PEST analysis (Political, Economic, Social, and Technological), STEER analysis (Socio-cultural, Technological, Economic, Ecological, and Regulatory factors), and EPISTEL .

Strategic planning is the formal consideration of an organization`s future course. All Strategic planning deals with at least one of three key questions:

· `What do we do?`

· `For whom do we do it?`

· `How do we excel?`

In business Strategic planning, the third question is better phrased `How can we beat or avoid competition?`.

Market requirements document

A market requirements document in project management and systems engineering, is a document that express the customer`s wants and needs for the product or service.

Resources

A resource is any physical or virtual entity of limited availability, or anything used to help one earn a living. In most cases, commercial or even ethic factors require resource allocation through resource management.

As resources are very useful, we attach some information value to them.

Concepts

Kant declared that human minds possess pure or a priori concepts. Instead of being abstracted from individual perceptions, like empirical concepts, they originate in the mind itself. He called these concepts categories, in the sense of the word that means predicate, attribute, characteristic, or quality.

Capital structure

In finance, Capital structure refers to the way a corporation finances its assets through some combination of equity, debt, a firm that sells $20 billion in equity and $80 billion in debt is said to be 20% equity-financed and 80% debt-financed.

Models

Experience curve re-directs here. For its use in video games see Experience point.

Models of the learning curve effect and the closely related experience curve effect express the relationship between equations for experience and efficiency or between efficiency gains and investment in the effort.

Chapter 2. TECHNOLOGICAL INNOVATION AND STRATEGY

Vertical integration	In microeconomics and management, the term Vertical integration describes a style of management control. Vertically integrated companies in a supply chain are united through a common owner. Usually each member of the supply chain produces a different product or (market-specific) service, and the products combine to satisfy a common need.
File sharing	File sharing is the practice of distributing or providing access to digitally stored information, such as computer programs, multi-media (audio, video), documents, transmission, and distribution models. Common methods are manual sharing using removable media, centralized computer file server installations on computer networks, World Wide Web-based hyperlinked documents, and the use of distributed peer-to-peer (P2P) networking.
Communications management	Communications management is the systematic planning, implementing, monitoring, and revision of all the channels of communication within an organization, and between organizations; it also includes the organization and dissemination of new communication directives connected with an organization, network, designing internal and external communications directives, and managing the flow of information, including online communication. New technology forces constant innovation on the part of communications managers.
Time Warner	Time Warner Inc. (NYSE: Time Warner X) is the world`s third largest media and entertainment conglomerate by market capitalization (behind News Corporation, headquartered in the Time Warner Center in New York City. (TimeWarner.com Fact Sheet Page) Formerly three separate companies (and owns the assets of a fourth, Turner Broadcasting System, Inc., acquired by a pre-AOL merger Time Warner in 1996): Warner Communications, Inc.
Gold Star	The Gold Star medal is a special insignia that identifies recipients of the title `Hero` in the Soviet Union and several post-Soviet states. The Gold Star was established by the decree of the Presidium of the Supreme Soviet on August 1, 1939. Previously, Heroes of the Soviet Union were awarded the Order of Lenin and a special diploma (gramota, Ð³Ñ€Ð°Ð¼Ð¾Ñ‚Ð°) describing the heroic feat. The medal was introduced to distinguish these heroes from other Order of Lenin recipients.
Electronic data interchange	Electronic Data Interchange refers to the structured transmission of data between organizations by electronic means. It is used to transfer electronic documents from one computer system to another, i.e. from one trading partner to another trading partner. It is more than mere E-mail; for instance, organizations might replace bills of lading and even checks with appropriate Electronic Data Interchange messages.
Four Ps	The four main fields of the Marketing mix.

The marketing mix is generally accepted as the use and specification of the `Four Ps` describing the strategy position of a product in the marketplace. The `marketing mix` is a set of controllable, tactical marketing tools that work together to achieve company`s objectives. One version of the marketing mix originated in 1948 when James Culliton said that a marketing decision should be a result of something similar to a recipe.

Commander

Commander is a naval rank which is also sometimes used as a military title depending on the individual customs of a given military service. Commander is also used as a rank or title in some organizations outside of the armed forces, particularly in police and law enforcement.

Commander is a rank used in many navies and some air forces but is very rarely used as a rank in armies, but is a common rank in special forces as it refers to a team leader.

Sunk costs

In economics and business decision-making, Sunk costs are retrospective (past) costs that have already been incurred and cannot be recovered. Sunk costs are sometimes contrasted with prospective costs, which are future costs that may be incurred or changed if an action is taken. Both retrospective and prospective costs may be either fixed (that is, they are not dependent on the volume of economic activity, however measured) or variable (dependent on volume).

Demographic profile

Demographic profile is a term used in marketing and broadcasting, to describe a demographic grouping or a market segment. This typically involves age bands , social class bands and gender.

A Demographic profile can be used to determine when and where advertising should be placed so as to achieve maximum results.

Synthetic environment

Synthetic environment refers to simulations on the internet that represent activities at a high level of realism, from simulations of theaters of war to factories and manufacturing processes. These environments may be created within a single computer or a vast distributed network connected by local and wide area networks and augmented by super-realistic special effects and accurate behavioral models. Synthetic environment allows visualization of and immersion into the environment being simulated.

The Synthetic environment could be divided into the terms below to eliminate ambiguity and confusion:

	· Synthetic natural environment - Representation of climate, weather, terrain, oceans, space, etc. · Synthetic human-made environment - Representation of human-made structures like buildings, bridges, and roads · Synthetic psychological environment - Representation of psychological influences on individuals and/or groups based on demography and other cultural factors.
Vivendi SA	Vivendi SA is a French international media conglomerate with activities in music, television and film, publishing, telecommunications, the Internet, and video games. On December 14, 1853, a water company named Compagnie Générale des Eaux (CGE) was created by an Imperial decree of Napoleon III. In 1854, CGE obtained a concession in order to supply water to the public in Lyon, serving in this capacity for over a hundred years.
Distribution	Distribution (or place) is one of the four elements of marketing mix. An organization or set of organizations (go-betweens) involved in the process of making a product or service available for use or consumption by a consumer or business user. The other three parts of the marketing mix are product, pricing, and promotion.
Market segmentation	Market segmentation is a concept in economics and marketing. A market segment is a sub-set of a market made up of people or organizations sharing with one or more characteristics that cause them to demand similar product and/or services based on qualities of those products such as price or function. A true market segment meets all of the following criteria: it is distinct from other segments (different segments have different needs), it is homogeneous within the segment (exhibits common needs); it responds similarly to a market stimulus, and it can be reached by a market intervention.
Competition	Co-operative Competition is based upon promoting mutual survival - \`everyone wins\`. Adam Smith\`s \`invisible hand\` is a process where individuals compete to improve their level of happiness but compete in a cooperative manner through peaceful exchange and without violating other people. Cooperative Competition focuses individuals/groups/organisms against the environment.
Single version of the truth	In computerized business management, Single version of the truth is a technical concept describing the data warehousing ideal of having either a single centralised database, or at least a distributed synchronised database, which stores all of an organisation\`s data in a consistent and non-redundant form.

In some systems and in the context of message processing systems (often realtime systems), this term also refers to the goal of establishing a single agreed sequence of messages within a database formed by a particular but arbitrary sequencing of records. The key concept is that data combined in a certain sequence is a `truth` which may be analyzed and processed giving particular results, and that although the sequence is arbitrary (and thus another correct but equally arbitrary sequencing would ultimately provide different results in any analysis), it is desirable to agree that the sequence enshrined in the `Single version of the truth` is the version that will be considered `the truth`, and that any conclusions drawn from analysis of the database are valid and unarguable, and (in a technical context) the database may be duplicated to a backup environment to ensure a persistent record is kept of the `Single version of the truth`.

E-commerce

Electronic commerce, commonly known as (electronic marketing) e-commerce or eCommerce, consists of the buying and selling of products or services over electronic systems such as the Internet and other computer networks. The amount of trade conducted electronically has grown extraordinarily with widespread Internet usage. The use of commerce is conducted in this way, spurring and drawing on innovations in electronic funds transfer, supply chain management, Internet marketing, online transaction processing, electronic data interchange (EDI), inventory management systems, and automated data collection systems.

Personalized

Personalization involves using technology to accommodate the differences between individuals. Once confined mainly to the Web, it is increasingly becoming a factor in education, healthcare (i.e. personalized medicine), and both `business to business` and `business to consumer` settings.

.

Economic value

The Economic value of a good or service has puzzled economists since the beginning of the discipline. First, economists tried to estimate the value of a good to an individual alone, and extend that definition to goods which can be exchanged. From this analysis came the concepts value in use and value in exchange.Wealth maximization predicts that a person will choose to obtain the good or service in the place where it is cheapest, where the amount given up is the least.Value is linked to price through the mechanism of exchange. When an economist observes an exchange, two important value functions are revealed: those of the buyer and seller. Just as the buyer reveals what he is willing to pay for a certain amount of a good, so too does the seller reveal what it costs him to give up the good.

Value chain

The Value chain is a concept from business management that was first described and popularized by Michael Porter in his 1985 best-seller, Competitive Advantage: Creating and Sustaining Superior Performance.

A Value chain is a chain of activities for a firm operating in a specific industry. The business unit is the appropriate level for construction of a Value chain, not the divisional level or corporate level.

GameSpot

GameSpot is a video gaming website that provides news, reviews, previews, downloads, and other information. The site was launched in May 1996 by Pete Deemer, Vince Broady and Jon Epstein. It was purchased by ZDNet, a brand which was later purchased by CNET Networks.

Gawker Media

Gawker Media is an online media company founded and owned by Nick Denton based in New York City. It is considered to be one of the most visible and successful blog-oriented media companies. As of January 2009, it is the parent company for 10 different weblogs, including Gawker.com, Defamer, Fleshbot, Deadspin, Lifehacker, Gizmodo, io9, Kotaku, Jalopnik, and Jezebel.

Marketing

Marketing is a `social and managerial process by which individuals and groups obtain what they need and want through creating and exchanging products and values with others.` It is an integrated process through which companies create value for customers and build strong customer relationships in order to capture value from customers in return.

marketing is used to create the customer, to keep the customer and to satisfy the customer. With the customer as the focus of its activities, it can be concluded that marketing management is one of the major components of business management.

Enpocket

Enpocket is a global mobile media company providing integrated entertainment and mobile marketing services. The company was founded in 2001, is headquartered in Boston, Massachusetts and since 2007 operates as a subsidiary of Nokia.

Solutions include:

· Enpocket Platform: a mobile campaign management and delivery system combining multi-modal mechanics, including SMS, MMS, WAP advertising, and video with predictive analytics

· Enpocket Mechanics: used by advertisers to lead consumers to store, to sell tickets, to offer ring tones and wallpapers, to offer discount coupons, and to show video of a product in action

	· Enpocket Network: provides brands to reach audience.
Revenue	In business, Revenue is income that a company receives from its normal business activities, usually from the sale of goods and services to customers. In many countries, such as the United Kingdom, Revenue is referred to as turnover. Some companies receive Revenue from interest, dividends or royalties paid to them by other companies.
Revenue sharing	Revenue sharing has multiple, related meanings depending on context. In business, Revenue sharing refers to the sharing of profits and losses among different groups. One form shares between the general partner(s) and limited partners in a limited partnership. Another form shares with a company`s employees, and another between companies in a business alliance.
Value based pricing	Value based pricing is a business strategy. It sets selling prices on the perceived value to the customer, rather than on the actual cost of the product, the market price, competitors prices, or the historical price. The goal of Value based pricing is to align price with value delivered. Price for any individual customer can be customized to reflect the specific value delivered. Examples could include metrics such as number of users and the value per users, number of annual transactions and the value per transaction, size of revenues and the impact on revenues, cost savings, or other measurements. Value based pricing is intended to make companies become more competitive and more profitable than using simpler pricing methods. It can also be used in product development and product management to configure products to maximize value for specific customers.Value-based pricing is dependent upon an understanding of how customers measure value, through careful
Product placement	Product placement, is a form of advertisement, where branded goods or services are placed in a context usually devoid of ads, such as movies, the story line of television shows, or news programs. The product placement is often not disclosed at the time that the good or service is featured. product placement became common in the 1980s.

Incident management	Incident management refers to the activities of an organization to identify, analyze and correct hazards. For instance, a fire in a factory would be a risk that realized, or an incident that happened. An Incident Response Team (IRT) or an Incident management Team (IMT), specifically designated for the task beforehand or on the spot, would then manage the organization through the incident.
Research and development	The phrase Research and development according to the Organization for Economic Co-operation and Development, refers to `creative work undertaken on a systematic basis in order to increase the stock of knowledge, including knowledge of man, culture and society, and the use of this stock of knowledge to devise new applications`. New product design and development is more often than not a crucial factor in the survival of a company. In an industry that is fast changing, firms must continually revise their design and range of products.
Xerox	Xerox Corporation is a global document management company which manufactures and sells a range of color and black-and-white printers, multifunction systems, photo copiers, digital production printing presses, and related consulting services and supplies. Xerox is headquartered in Norwalk, Connecticut , though its largest population of employees is based in and around Rochester, New York, the area in which the company was founded. The Xerox 914 was the first one-piece plain paper photocopier, and sold in the thousands. Xerox was founded in 1906 in Rochester, New York as `The Haloid Company`, which originally manufactured photographic paper and equipment.
Job rotation	Job rotation is an approach to management development where an individual is moved through a schedule of assignments designed to give him or her a breadth of exposure to the entire operation. Job rotation is also practiced to allow qualified employees to gain more insights into the processes of a company, and to reduce boredom and increase job satisfaction through job variation. The term Job rotation can also mean the scheduled exchange of persons in offices, especially in public offices, prior to the end of incumbency or the legislative period.

Funding	Funding or financing is to provide capital (funds), which means resources, usually in form of money, for a project, a person, a business or any other private or public institutions. When a request f is made then fundraising is being attempted. Those funds can be allocated for either short term or long term purposes.
Employment	Employment is a contract between two parties, one being the employer and the other being the employee. An employee may be defined as: \`A person in the service of another under any contract of hire, express or implied, oral or written, where the employer has the power or right to control and direct the employee in the material details of how the work is to be performed.\` Black\`s Law Dictionary page 471 (5th ed. 1979). In a commercial setting, the employer conceives of a productive activity, generally with the intention of generating a profit, and the employee contributes labour to the enterprise, usually in return for payment of wages.
Tolerance	Toleration and Tolerance are terms used in social, cultural and religious contexts to describe attitudes which are \`tolerant\` (or moderately respectful) of practices or group memberships that may be disapproved of by those in the majority. In practice, Tolerance indicates support for practices that prohibit ethnic and religious discrimination. Conversely, \`in Tolerance \` may be used to refer to the discriminatory practices sought to be prohibited.
Competitive advantage	Competitive advantage is a position of a company in a competitive landscape that allows the company earning return on investments higher than the cost of investments. Competitive advantage should be relevant, unique, and sustainable. Competitive advantage is a theory that seeks to address some of the criticisms of comparative advantage.
Strategic business unit	Strategic business unit is understood as a business unit within the overall corporate identity which is distinguishable from other business because it serves a defined external market where management can conduct strategic planning in relation to products and markets. The unique small business unit benefits that a firm aggressively promotes in a consistent manner. When companies become really large, they are best thought of as being composed of a number of businesses (or Strategic business units).

Leadership	In response to the criticism of the trait approach, theorists began to research Leadership as a set of behaviors, evaluating the behavior of `successful` leaders, determining a behavior taxonomy and identifying broad Leadership styles. David McClelland, for example, saw Leadership skills, not so much as a set of traits, but as a pattern of motives. He claimed that successful leaders will tend to have a high need for power, a low need for affiliation, and a high level of what he called activity inhibition (one might call it self-control).

Chapter 3. TECHNOLOGICAL EVOLUTION

Case study	A Case study is one of several ways of doing research whether it is social science related or even socially related. It is an intensive study of a single group, incident, or community. Other ways include experiments, surveys, or analysis of archival information.
Innovation	Innovation is a change in the thought process for doing something or `new stuff that is made useful`. It may refer to an incremental emergent or radical and revolutionary changes in thinking, products, processes, or organizations. Following Schumpeter (1934), contributors to the scholarly literature on Innovation typically distinguish between invention, an idea made manifest, and Innovation, ideas applied successfully in practice.
Six Sigma	Six Sigma is a business management strategy originally developed by Motorola, USA in 1981. As of 2010, it enjoys widespread application in many sectors of industry, although its application is not without controversy. Six Sigma seeks to improve the quality of process outputs by identifying and removing the causes of defects (errors) and minimizing variability in manufacturing and business processes. It uses a set of quality management methods, including statistical methods, and creates a special infrastructure of people within the organization (`Black Belts`, `Green Belts`, etc).
Market dominance	Market dominance is a measure of the strength of a brand, product, service, relative to competitive offerings. There is often a geographic element to the competitive landscape. In defining Market dominance, you must see to what extent a product, brand, or firm controls a product category in a given geographic area.
Market	A Market is any one of a variety of different systems, institutions, procedures, social relations and infrastructures whereby persons trade, and goods and services are exchanged, forming part of the economy. It is an arrangement that allows buyers and sellers to exchange things. Markets vary in size, range, geographic scale, location, types and variety of human communities, as well as the types of goods and services traded.
File sharing	File sharing is the practice of distributing or providing access to digitally stored information, such as computer programs, multi-media (audio, video), documents, transmission, and distribution models. Common methods are manual sharing using removable media, centralized computer file server installations on computer networks, World Wide Web-based hyperlinked documents, and the use of distributed peer-to-peer (P2P) networking.
Nominative determinism	Nominative determinism refers to the theory that a person`s name is given an influential role in reflecting key attributes of his job, profession, but real examples are more highly prized, the more obscure the better.

Chapter 3. TECHNOLOGICAL EVOLUTION

Innovation Management	Innovation management is the discipline of managing processes in innovation. It can be used to develop both product and organizational innovation. Without proper processes, it is not possible for R'D to be efficient; Innovation management includes a set of tools that allow managers and engineers to cooperate with a common understanding of goals and processes.
Concepts	Kant declared that human minds possess pure or a priori concepts. Instead of being abstracted from individual perceptions, like empirical concepts, they originate in the mind itself. He called these concepts categories, in the sense of the word that means predicate, attribute, characteristic, or quality.
Market development	A Market development strategy targets non-buying customers in currently targeted segments. It also targets new customers in new segments. A marketing manager has to think about the following questions before implementing a Market development strategy: Is it profitable? Will it require the introduction of new or modified products? Is the customer and channel well enough researched and understood? The marketing manager uses these four groups to give more focus to the market segment decision: existing customers, competitor customers, non-buying in current segments, new segments.
Probability density function	In probability theory, a Probability density function of a continuous random variable is a function that describes the relative likelihood for this random variable to occur at a given point in the observation space. The probability of a random variable falling within a given set is given by the integral of its density over the set. The terms `probability distribution function` and `probability function` have also been used to denote the Probability density function.
Electronic Business	Electronic business may be defined as the utilization of information and communication technologies (ICT) in support of all the activities of business. Commerce constitutes the exchange of products and services between businesses, groups and individuals and can be seen as one of the essential activities of any business. Electronic commerce focuses on the use of ICT to enable the external activities and relationships of the business with individuals, groups and other businesses.

Chapter 3. TECHNOLOGICAL EVOLUTION

Competitiveness	Competitiveness is a comparative concept of the ability and performance of a firm, sub-sector or country to sell and supply goods and/or services in a given market. Although widely used in economics and business management, the usefulness of the concept, particularly in the context of national competitiveness, is vigorously disputed by economists, such as Paul Krugman . The term may also be applied to markets, where it is used to refer to the extent to which the market structure may be regarded as perfectly competitive.
Business model	A Business model describes the rationale of how an organization creates, delivers, and captures value - economic, social, or other forms of value. The process of Business model design is part of business strategy. In theory and practice the term Business model is used for a broad range of informal and formal descriptions to represent core aspects of a business, including purpose, offerings, strategies, infrastructure, organizational structures, trading practices, and operational processes and policies.
Single version of the truth	In computerized business management, Single version of the truth is a technical concept describing the data warehousing ideal of having either a single centralised database, or at least a distributed synchronised database, which stores all of an organisation`s data in a consistent and non-redundant form. In some systems and in the context of message processing systems (often realtime systems), this term also refers to the goal of establishing a single agreed sequence of messages within a database formed by a particular but arbitrary sequencing of records. The key concept is that data combined in a certain sequence is a `truth` which may be analyzed and processed giving particular results, and that although the sequence is arbitrary (and thus another correct but equally arbitrary sequencing would ultimately provide different results in any analysis), it is desirable to agree that the sequence enshrined in the `Single version of the truth` is the version that will be considered `the truth`, and that any conclusions drawn from analysis of the database are valid and unarguable, and (in a technical context) the database may be duplicated to a backup environment to ensure a persistent record is kept of the `Single version of the truth`.
Models	Experience curve re-directs here. For its use in video games see Experience point. Models of the learning curve effect and the closely related experience curve effect express the relationship between equations for experience and efficiency or between efficiency gains and investment in the effort.

Business value

In management, Business value is an informal term that includes all forms of value that determine the health and well-being of the firm in the long-run. Business value expands concept of value of the firm beyond economic value (also known as economic profit, Economic value added, and Shareholder value) to include other forms of value such as employee value, customer value, supplier value, channel partner value, alliance partner value, managerial value, and societal value. Many of these forms of value are not directly measured in monetary terms.

Marketing

Marketing is a `social and managerial process by which individuals and groups obtain what they need and want through creating and exchanging products and values with others.` It is an integrated process through which companies create value for customers and build strong customer relationships in order to capture value from customers in return.

marketing is used to create the customer, to keep the customer and to satisfy the customer. With the customer as the focus of its activities, it can be concluded that marketing management is one of the major components of business management.

Communications management

Communications management is the systematic planning, implementing, monitoring, and revision of all the channels of communication within an organization, and between organizations; it also includes the organization and dissemination of new communication directives connected with an organization, network, designing internal and external communications directives, and managing the flow of information, including online communication. New technology forces constant innovation on the part of communications managers.

Competition

Co-operative Competition is based upon promoting mutual survival - `everyone wins`. Adam Smith`s `invisible hand` is a process where individuals compete to improve their level of happiness but compete in a cooperative manner through peaceful exchange and without violating other people. Cooperative Competition focuses individuals/groups/organisms against the environment.

Barriers to entry

In economics and mostly especially in the theory of competition, Barriers to entry are obstacles in the path of a firm that make it difficult to enter a given market.

Barriers to entry protect incumbant firms from competition from newcomers.

Barriers to entry are the source of a firm`s pricing power - the ability of a firm to raise prices without losing all its customers.

Evaluation	Evaluation is systematic determination of merit, worth, and significance of something or someone using criteria against a set of standards. Evaluation often is used to characterize and appraise subjects of interest in a wide range of human enterprises, including the arts, criminal justice, foundations and non-profit organizations, government, health care, and other human services.
Group	In business, a group, business group, corporate group) alliance is most commonly a legal entity that is a type of conglomerate or holding company consisting of a parent company and subsidiaries. Typical examples are Adidas group or Icelandair group. In United Arab Emirates, Business group can also be knows as Trade association.
Software Testing	Software testing is an investigation conducted to provide stakeholders with information about the quality of the product or service under test. Software testing also provides an objective, independent view of the software to allow the business to appreciate and understand the risks at implementation of the software. Test techniques include, but are not limited to, the process of executing a program or application with the intent of finding software bugs. Software testing can also be stated as the process of validating and verifying that a software program/application/product: · meets the business and technical requirements that guided its design and development; · works as expected; and · can be implemented with the same characteristics Software testing, depending on the testing method employed, can be implemented at any time in the development process.
Niche market	A Niche market is the subset of the market on which a specific product is focusing; therefore the market niche defines the specific product features aimed at satisfying specific market needs, as well as the price range, production quality and the demographics that is intended to impact. Every single product that is on sale can be defined by its Niche market. As of special note, the products aimed at a wide demographic audience, with the resulting low price , are said to belong to the mainstream niche--in practice referred to only as mainstream or of high demand.

Chapter 3. TECHNOLOGICAL EVOLUTION

Revenue	In business, Revenue is income that a company receives from its normal business activities, usually from the sale of goods and services to customers. In many countries, such as the United Kingdom, Revenue is referred to as turnover. Some companies receive Revenue from interest, dividends or royalties paid to them by other companies.
Motivation	Motivation is the activation or energization of goal-oriented behavior. Motivation may be internal or external. The term is generally used for humans but, theoretically, it can also be used to describe the causes for animal behavior as well.
Hostile work environment	A Hostile work environment exists when an employee experiences workplace harassment and fears going to work because of the offensive, intimidating, religion, sex, national origin, age, disability, veteran status, or, in some jurisdictions, sexual orientation, political affiliation, citizenship status, marital status, or personal appearance. Hostile work environment is also one of the two legal categories of sexual harassment. A Hostile work environment may also be defined as when a boss or manager begins to engage in a manner designed to make you quit in retaliation for your actions.
Xerox	Xerox Corporation is a global document management company which manufactures and sells a range of color and black-and-white printers, multifunction systems, photo copiers, digital production printing presses, and related consulting services and supplies. Xerox is headquartered in Norwalk, Connecticut , though its largest population of employees is based in and around Rochester, New York, the area in which the company was founded. The Xerox 914 was the first one-piece plain paper photocopier, and sold in the thousands. Xerox was founded in 1906 in Rochester, New York as `The Haloid Company`, which originally manufactured photographic paper and equipment.
Asset	In financial accounting, Assets are economic resources. Anything tangible or intangible that is capable of being owned or controlled to produce value and that is held to have positive economic value is considered an Asset. Simplistically stated, Assets represent ownership of value that can be converted into cash (although cash itself is also considered an Asset).
Complementary assets	Complementary assets are assets, infrastructure or capabilities needed to support the successful commercialization and marketing of a technological innovation, other than those assets fundamentally associated with that innovation. The term was first coined by David Teece. Key empirical studies on Complementary assets were conducted by Frank T. Rothaermel. Complementary assets are broken down into three general types:

· Generic assets: `general purpose` assets which do not need to be tailored to a particular innovation;

· Specialized assets: unilateral dependence between the innovation and the complementary asset;

· Cospecialized assets: bilateral dependence between the innovation and the complementary asset.

Disruptive innovation	Disruptive innovation is a term used in business and technology literature to describe innovations that improve a product or service in ways that the market does not expect, typically by lowering price or designing for a different set of consumers. In contrast to `Disruptive innovation`, a `sustaining` innovation does not have an effect on existing markets. Sustaining innovations may be either `discontinuous` (i.e. `transformational`) or `continuous` (i.e. `evolutionary`).
Economic value	The Economic value of a good or service has puzzled economists since the beginning of the discipline. First, economists tried to estimate the value of a good to an individual alone, and extend that definition to goods which can be exchanged. From this analysis came the concepts value in use and value in exchange.Wealth maximization predicts that a person will choose to obtain the good or service in the place where it is cheapest, where the amount given up is the least.Value is linked to price through the mechanism of exchange. When an economist observes an exchange, two important value functions are revealed: those of the buyer and seller. Just as the buyer reveals what he is willing to pay for a certain amount of a good, so too does the seller reveal what it costs him to give up the good.
Capital structure	In finance, Capital structure refers to the way a corporation finances its assets through some combination of equity, debt, a firm that sells $20 billion in equity and $80 billion in debt is said to be 20% equity-financed and 80% debt-financed.
Litmus	Litmus is a water-soluble mixture of different dyes extracted from lichens, especially Roccella tinctoria. It is often absorbed onto filter paper to produce one of the oldest forms of pH indicator, used to test materials for acidity. Blue Litmus paper turns red under acidic conditions and red Litmus paper turns blue under basic (i.e. alkaline) conditions with the color change occurring over the pH range 4.5-8.3 at 25 °C. Neutral Litmus paper is purple in color.

Generalized additive model

In statistics, the Generalized additive model is a statistical model developed by Trevor Hastie and Rob Tibshirani for blending properties of generalized linear models with additive models.

The model specifies a distribution (such as a normal distribution, or a binomial distribution) and a link function g relating the expected value of the distribution to the predictors, and attempts to fit functions f_i to satisfy:

$$g(\mathrm{E}(Y)) = \beta_0 + f_1(x_1) + f_2(x_2) + \cdots + f_m(x_m).$$

The functions $f_i(x_i)$ may be fit using parametric or non-parametric means, thus providing the potential for better fits to data than other methods. The method hence is very general - a typical Generalized additive model might use a scatterplot smoothing function such as a locally weighted mean for $f_1(x_1)$, and then use a factor model for $f_2(x_2)$. By allowing nonparametric fits, well designed Generalized additive models allow good fits to the training data with relaxed assumptions on the actual relationship, perhaps at the expense of interpretability of results.

Purdue University College of Consumer and Family Sciences

The Purdue University College of Consumer and Family Sciences is one of eight major academic divisions, of Purdue University. All of the college`s teaching and research activities center on issues related to family and consumer science. Its Hospitality and Tourism Management program has been ranked first in the United States.
The College of Consumer and Family Sciences contains an interdisciplinary program in Consumer and Family Sciences Education and four minor academic divisions, or Departments:

· Child Development and Family Studies

· Consumer Sciences and Retailing

· Foods and Nutrition

· Hospitality and Tourism Management

The College of Consumer and Family Sciences is distributed across three main buildings.

Retailing	Retailing consists of the sale of goods or merchandise from a fixed location, such as a department store, boutique or kiosk, in small or individual lots for direct consumption by the purchaser. Retailing may include subordinated services, such as delivery. Purchasers may be individuals or businesses.
Camera	A Camera is a device that records images, either as a still photograph or as moving images known as videos or movies. The term comes from the Camera obscura , an early mechanism of projecting images where an entire room functioned as a real-time imaging system; the modern Camera evolved from the Camera obscura. Cameras may work with the light of the visible spectrum or with other portions of the electromagnetic spectrum.
Modularity	Modularity is a general systems concept, typically defined as a continuum describing the degree to which a system`s components may be separated and recombined. It refers to both the tightness of coupling between components, and the degree to which the `rules` of the system architecture enable the mixing and matching of components.
Disposable	A disposable is a product designed for cheapness and short-term convenience rather than medium to long-term durability, with most products only intended for single use. The term is also sometimes used for products that may last several months (ex. disposable air filters) to distinguish from similar products that last indefinitely (ex.
Demand	In economics, Demand is the desire to own anything and the ability to pay for it and willigness to pay . The term Demand signifies the ability or the willingness to buy a particular commodity at a given point of time. Demand is also defined elsewhere as a measure of preferences that is weighted by income.
Enterprise resource planning	Enterprise resource planning is an Integrated computer-based system used to manage internal and external resources, including tangible assets, financial resources, materials, and human resources. It is a software architecture whose purpose is to facilitate the flow of information between all business functions inside the boundaries of the organization and manage the connections to outside stakeholders. Built on a centralized database and normally utilizing a common computing platform, Enterprise resource planning systems consolidate all business operations into a uniform and enterprise-wide system environment.

Resource allocation	Resource allocation is used to assign the available resources in an economic way. It is part of resource management. In project management, Resource allocation is the scheduling of activities and the resources required by those activities while taking into consideration both the resource availability and the project time.
Resource dependence	The procurement of external resources is an important tenet of both the strategic and tactical management of any company. Nevertheless, a theory of the consequences of this importance was not formalized until the 1970s, with the publication of The External Control of Organizations: A resource dependence Perspective (Pfeffer and Salancik 1978). resource dependence Theory (RDT) has implications regarding the optimal divisional structure of organizations, recruitment of board members and employees, production strategies, contract structure, external organizational links, and many other aspects of organizational strategy.
Venture capital	Venture capital is provided as seed funding to early-stage, high-potential, growth companies and more often after the seed funding round as growth funding round (also referred as series A round) in the interest of generating a return through an eventual realization event such as an IPO or trade sale of the company. To put it simply, an investment firm will give money to a growing company. The growing company will then use this money to advertise, do research, build infrastructure, develop products etc.
Vertical integration	In microeconomics and management, the term Vertical integration describes a style of management control. Vertically integrated companies in a supply chain are united through a common owner. Usually each member of the supply chain produces a different product or (market-specific) service, and the products combine to satisfy a common need.
Competitive advantage	Competitive advantage is a position of a company in a competitive landscape that allows the company earning return on investments higher than the cost of investments. Competitive advantage should be relevant, unique, and sustainable. Competitive advantage is a theory that seeks to address some of the criticisms of comparative advantage.

Transaction cost	In economics and related disciplines, a Transaction cost is a cost incurred in making an economic exchange (restated: the cost of participating in a market.) For example, most people, when buying or selling a stock, must pay a commission to their broker; that commission is a Transaction cost of doing the stock deal. Or consider buying a banana from a store; to purchase the banana, your costs will be not only the price of the banana itself, but also the energy and effort it requires to find out which of the various banana products you prefer, where to get them and at what price, the cost of traveling from your house to the store and back, the time waiting in line, and the effort of the paying itself; the costs above and beyond the cost of the banana are the Transaction cost s.
Efficiency ratio	The Efficiency ratio, a ratio that is typically applied to banks, in simple terms is defined as expenses as a percentage of revenue (expenses / revenue), with a few variations. A lower percentage is better since that means expenses are low and earnings are high. It is related to operating leverage, which measures the ratio between fixed costs and variable costs.
Advanced Micro Devices	Advanced Micro Devices, Inc. is an American multinational semiconductor company based in Sunnyvale, California, that develops computer processors and related technologies for commercial and consumer markets. Its main products include microprocessors, motherboard chipsets, embedded processors and graphics processors for servers, workstations and personal computers, and processor technologies for handheld devices, digital television, automobiles, game consoles, and other embedded systems applications.
Securitization	Securitization is a structured finance process that distributes risk by aggregating debt instruments in a pool, then issues new securities backed by the pool. The term \`Securitization\` is derived from the fact that the form of financial instruments used to obtain funds from the investors are securities. As a portfolio risk backed by amortizing cash flows - and unlike general corporate debt - the credit quality of securitized debt is non-stationary due to changes in volatility that are time- and structure-dependent.
Economic profit	In neoclassical economics, economic profit is the difference between a firm\`s total revenue and its opportunity costs. In classical economics profit is the return to the employer of capital stock in any productive pursuit involving labor. These two definitions are actually the same.
Time to market	In commerce, Time to market is the length of time it takes from a product being conceived until its being available for sale. Time to market is important in industries where products are outmoded quickly. A common assumption is that Time to market matters most for first-of-a-kind products, but actually the leader often has the luxury of time, while the clock is clearly running for the followers.

Chapter 4. INDUSTRY CONTEXT

Case study	A Case study is one of several ways of doing research whether it is social science related or even socially related. It is an intensive study of a single group, incident, or community. Other ways include experiments, surveys, or analysis of archival information.
Demand	In economics, Demand is the desire to own anything and the ability to pay for it and willigness to pay . The term Demand signifies the ability or the willingness to buy a particular commodity at a given point of time. Demand is also defined elsewhere as a measure of preferences that is weighted by income.
Market	A Market is any one of a variety of different systems, institutions, procedures, social relations and infrastructures whereby persons trade, and goods and services are exchanged, forming part of the economy. It is an arrangement that allows buyers and sellers to exchange things. Markets vary in size, range, geographic scale, location, types and variety of human communities, as well as the types of goods and services traded.
Communications management	Communications management is the systematic planning, implementing, monitoring, and revision of all the channels of communication within an organization, and between organizations; it also includes the organization and dissemination of new communication directives connected with an organization, network, designing internal and external communications directives, and managing the flow of information, including online communication. New technology forces constant innovation on the part of communications managers.
Southern New England Telecommunications	Southern New England Telecommunications Corporation started operations in 1986 as the holding company for The Southern New England Telephone Company. Prior to 1986, The Southern New England Telephone Company had been a minority holding of AT'T until February 1986, when AT'T withdrew its 23% holding. Southern New England Telecommunications then became its own company, operating a telecommunications sales division, Sonecor Systems Division, which began operations on January 1, 1983 and sold equipment in competition with AT'T before the Bell System divestiture.
US West	US West, Inc. was a Regional Bell Operating Company, one of seven `Baby Bells` that were spawned by the antitrust breakup of AT'T in 1983. It provided telephone and data service to several Pacific Northwest and mountain states. It was acquired by Qwest Communications International on June 30, 2000, in what some economists have charged as a hostile takeover.

File sharing	File sharing is the practice of distributing or providing access to digitally stored information, such as computer programs, multi-media (audio, video), documents, transmission, and distribution models. Common methods are manual sharing using removable media, centralized computer file server installations on computer networks, World Wide Web-based hyperlinked documents, and the use of distributed peer-to-peer (P2P) networking.
Group	In business, a group, business group, corporate group) alliance is most commonly a legal entity that is a type of conglomerate or holding company consisting of a parent company and subsidiaries. Typical examples are Adidas group or Icelandair group. In United Arab Emirates, Business group can also be knows as Trade association.
WorldCom	MCI, Inc. is an American telecommunications subsidiary of Verizon Communications that is headquartered in Ashburn, Virginia. The corporation was originally formed as a result of the merger of WorldCom and MCI Communications, and used the name MCI WorldCom followed by WorldCom before taking its final name on April 14, 2003 as part of the corporation`s emergence from bankruptcy.
Market dominance	Market dominance is a measure of the strength of a brand, product, service, relative to competitive offerings. There is often a geographic element to the competitive landscape. In defining Market dominance, you must see to what extent a product, brand, or firm controls a product category in a given geographic area.
Material flow	Material flow is the description of the transportation of raw materials, pre-fabricates, parts, components, integrated objects and finally products as a flow of entities. The term applies mainly to advanced modeling of Supply chain management. As industrial Material flow can easily become very complex Plant Simulation Software has been developed to simulate, visualize, analyze and optimize these processes.
Time Warner	Time Warner Inc. (NYSE: Time Warner X) is the world`s third largest media and entertainment conglomerate by market capitalization (behind News Corporation, headquartered in the Time Warner Center in New York City. (TimeWarner.com Fact Sheet Page) Formerly three separate companies (and owns the assets of a fourth, Turner Broadcasting System, Inc., acquired by a pre-AOL merger Time Warner in 1996): Warner Communications, Inc.
Competition	Co-operative Competition is based upon promoting mutual survival - `everyone wins`. Adam Smith`s `invisible hand` is a process where individuals compete to improve their level of happiness but compete in a cooperative manner through peaceful exchange and without violating other people. Cooperative Competition focuses individuals/groups/organisms against the environment.

Generalized additive model

In statistics, the Generalized additive model is a statistical model developed by Trevor Hastie and Rob Tibshirani for blending properties of generalized linear models with additive models.

The model specifies a distribution (such as a normal distribution, or a binomial distribution) and a link function g relating the expected value of the distribution to the predictors, and attempts to fit functions f_i to satisfy:

$$g(\mathrm{E}(Y)) = \beta_0 + f_1(x_1) + f_2(x_2) + \cdots + f_m(x_m).$$

The functions $f_i(x_i)$ may be fit using parametric or non-parametric means, thus providing the potential for better fits to data than other methods. The method hence is very general - a typical Generalized additive model might use a scatterplot smoothing function such as a locally weighted mean for $f_1(x_1)$, and then use a factor model for $f_2(x_2)$. By allowing nonparametric fits, well designed Generalized additive models allow good fits to the training data with relaxed assumptions on the actual relationship, perhaps at the expense of interpretability of results.

Management Consulting

Management consulting indicates both the industry of, and the practice of, helping organizations improve their performance, primarily through the analysis of existing business problems and development of plans for improvement.

Organizations hire the services of management consultants for a number of reasons, including gaining external (and presumably objective) advice and access to the consultants` specialized expertise.

Because of their exposure to and relationships with numerous organizations, consulting firms are also said to be aware of industry `best practices`, although the transferability of such practices from one organization to another may be limited or problematic.

Hostile work environment

A Hostile work environment exists when an employee experiences workplace harassment and fears going to work because of the offensive, intimidating, religion, sex, national origin, age, disability, veteran status, or, in some jurisdictions, sexual orientation, political affiliation, citizenship status, marital status, or personal appearance. Hostile work environment is also one of the two legal categories of sexual harassment.
A Hostile work environment may also be defined as when a boss or manager begins to engage in a manner designed to make you quit in retaliation for your actions.

Asset	In financial accounting, Assets are economic resources. Anything tangible or intangible that is capable of being owned or controlled to produce value and that is held to have positive economic value is considered an Asset. Simplistically stated, Assets represent ownership of value that can be converted into cash (although cash itself is also considered an Asset).
Complementary assets	Complementary assets are assets, infrastructure or capabilities needed to support the successful commercialization and marketing of a technological innovation, other than those assets fundamentally associated with that innovation. The term was first coined by David Teece. Key empirical studies on Complementary assets were conducted by Frank T. Rothaermel. Complementary assets are broken down into three general types: · Generic assets: \`general purpose\` assets which do not need to be tailored to a particular innovation; · Specialized assets: unilateral dependence between the innovation and the complementary asset; · Cospecialized assets: bilateral dependence between the innovation and the complementary asset.
Ownership	Ownership is the state or fact of exclusive rights and control over property, which may be an object, land/real estate or intellectual property. An Ownership right is also referred to as title. The concept of Ownership has existed for thousands of years and in all cultures.
Leadership	In response to the criticism of the trait approach, theorists began to research Leadership as a set of behaviors, evaluating the behavior of \`successful\` leaders, determining a behavior taxonomy and identifying broad Leadership styles. David McClelland, for example, saw Leadership skills, not so much as a set of traits, but as a pattern of motives. He claimed that successful leaders will tend to have a high need for power, a low need for affiliation, and a high level of what he called activity inhibition (one might call it self-control).
Difference in differences	Difference in differences is a nonexperimental technique used in econometrics that measures the effect of a treatment at a given period in time. It is often used to measure the change induced by a particular treatment or event, though may be subject to certain biases (mean reversion bias, etc)

The basic premise of `diff-in-diffs` is to examine the effect of some sort of treatment by comparing the treatment group after treatment both to the treatment group before treatment and to some other control group. Naively, you might consider simply looking at the treatment group before and after treatment to try to deduce the effect of the treatment.

Telemarketing

Telemarketing is a method of direct marketing in which a salesperson solicits to prospective customers to buy products or services, either over the phone or through a subsequent face to face or Web conferencing appointment scheduled during the call.
Telemarketing can also include recorded sales pitches programmed to be played over the phone via automatic dialing. Telemarketing has come under fire in recent years, being viewed as an annoyance by many.

Synthetic environment

Synthetic environment refers to simulations on the internet that represent activities at a high level of realism, from simulations of theaters of war to factories and manufacturing processes. These environments may be created within a single computer or a vast distributed network connected by local and wide area networks and augmented by super-realistic special effects and accurate behavioral models. Synthetic environment allows visualization of and immersion into the environment being simulated.

The Synthetic environment could be divided into the terms below to eliminate ambiguity and confusion:

· Synthetic natural environment - Representation of climate, weather, terrain, oceans, space, etc.

· Synthetic human-made environment - Representation of human-made structures like buildings, bridges, and roads

· Synthetic psychological environment - Representation of psychological influences on individuals and/or groups based on demography and other cultural factors.

Consultant

A Consultant is a professional who provides advice in a particular area of expertise such as management, accountancy, the environment, entertainment, technology, law (tax law, in particular), human resources, marketing, food production, medicine, finance, life management, economics, public affairs, communication, engineering, sound system design, graphic design, or waste management.

	A Consultant is usually an expert or a professional in a specific field and has a wide knowledge of the subject matter. A Consultant usually works for a consultancy firm or is self-employed, and engages with multiple and changing clients.
Procter ' Gamble	Procter is a surname, and may also refer to: · Bryan Waller Procter (pseud. Barry Cornwall), English poet · Goodwin Procter, American law firm · Procter ' Gamble, consumer products multinational `
Intellectual property	Intellectual property is a term referring to a number of distinct types of creations of the mind for which property rights are recognised--and the corresponding fields of law. Under Intellectual property law, owners are granted certain exclusive rights to a variety of intangible assets, such as musical, literary, and artistic works; discoveries and inventions; and words, phrases, symbols, and designs. Common types of Intellectual property include copyrights, trademarks, patents, industrial design rights and trade secrets in some jurisdictions.
Niche market	A Niche market is the subset of the market on which a specific product is focusing; therefore the market niche defines the specific product features aimed at satisfying specific market needs, as well as the price range, production quality and the demographics that is intended to impact. Every single product that is on sale can be defined by its Niche market. As of special note, the products aimed at a wide demographic audience, with the resulting low price , are said to belong to the mainstream niche--in practice referred to only as mainstream or of high demand.
Xerox	Xerox Corporation is a global document management company which manufactures and sells a range of color and black-and-white printers, multifunction systems, photo copiers, digital production printing presses, and related consulting services and supplies. Xerox is headquartered in Norwalk, Connecticut , though its largest population of employees is based in and around Rochester, New York, the area in which the company was founded. The Xerox 914 was the first one-piece plain paper photocopier, and sold in the thousands. Xerox was founded in 1906 in Rochester, New York as `The Haloid Company`, which originally manufactured photographic paper and equipment.

Single version of the truth	In computerized business management, Single version of the truth is a technical concept describing the data warehousing ideal of having either a single centralised database, or at least a distributed synchronised database, which stores all of an organisation`s data in a consistent and non-redundant form. In some systems and in the context of message processing systems (often realtime systems), this term also refers to the goal of establishing a single agreed sequence of messages within a database formed by a particular but arbitrary sequencing of records. The key concept is that data combined in a certain sequence is a `truth` which may be analyzed and processed giving particular results, and that although the sequence is arbitrary (and thus another correct but equally arbitrary sequencing would ultimately provide different results in any analysis), it is desirable to agree that the sequence enshrined in the `Single version of the truth` is the version that will be considered `the truth`, and that any conclusions drawn from analysis of the database are valid and unarguable, and (in a technical context) the database may be duplicated to a backup environment to ensure a persistent record is kept of the `Single version of the truth`.
Models	Experience curve re-directs here. For its use in video games see Experience point. Models of the learning curve effect and the closely related experience curve effect express the relationship between equations for experience and efficiency or between efficiency gains and investment in the effort.
Copyright	Copyright is the set of exclusive rights granted to the author or creator of an original work, including the right to copy, distribute and adapt the work. These rights can be licensed, transferred and/or assigned. Copyright lasts for a certain time period after which the work is said to enter the public domain.
Digital distribution	Digital distribution is the practice of delivering content without the use of physical media, typically by downloading via the internet straight to a consumer`s home. Digital distribution bypasses conventional physical distribution media, such as paper or DVDs. The term Digital distribution is typically applied to freestanding products; digital add-ons for other products are more commonly known as downloadable content.
Incident management	Incident management refers to the activities of an organization to identify, analyze and correct hazards. For instance, a fire in a factory would be a risk that realized, or an incident that happened. An Incident Response Team (IRT) or an Incident management Team (IMT), specifically designated for the task beforehand or on the spot, would then manage the organization through the incident.

Enterprise manufacturing intelligence	Enterprise manufacturing intelligence is a term which applies to software used to bring a corporation`s manufacturing-related data together from many sources for the purposes of reporting, analysis, visual summaries, and passing data between enterprise-level and plant-floor systems. As data is combined from multiple sources, it can be given a new structure or context that will help users find what they need regardless of where it came from. The primary goal is to turn large amounts of manufacturing data into real knowledge and drive business results based on that knowledge.
Market segmentation	Market segmentation is a concept in economics and marketing. A market segment is a sub-set of a market made up of people or organizations sharing with one or more characteristics that cause them to demand similar product and/or services based on qualities of those products such as price or function. A true market segment meets all of the following criteria: it is distinct from other segments (different segments have different needs), it is homogeneous within the segment (exhibits common needs); it responds similarly to a market stimulus, and it can be reached by a market intervention.
Vivendi SA	Vivendi SA is a French international media conglomerate with activities in music, television and film, publishing, telecommunications, the Internet, and video games. On December 14, 1853, a water company named Compagnie Générale des Eaux (CGE) was created by an Imperial decree of Napoleon III. In 1854, CGE obtained a concession in order to supply water to the public in Lyon, serving in this capacity for over a hundred years.
ELab	ELab is INSEAD`s center of excellence, a Think Tank for thought leadership, community outreach and value creation in the knowledge economy, founded in 2001 by the Roland Berger chaired Prof. Soumitra Dutta.  `eLab@INSEAD represents INSEAD`s commitment to cultivating and disseminating management knowledge and thought leadership with a focus on the digital economy.
Music video	A Music video is a short film or video that accompanies a complete piece of music/song. Modern Music videos are primarily made and used as a marketing device intended to promote the sale of music recordings. Although the origins of Music videos go back much further, they came into their own in the 1980s, when MTV based their format around the medium, and later with the launch of VH1. The term `Music video` first came into popular usage in the early 1980s.

Innovation

Innovation is a change in the thought process for doing something or `new stuff that is made useful`. It may refer to an incremental emergent or radical and revolutionary changes in thinking, products, processes, or organizations. Following Schumpeter (1934), contributors to the scholarly literature on Innovation typically distinguish between invention, an idea made manifest, and Innovation, ideas applied successfully in practice.

Revenue

In business, Revenue is income that a company receives from its normal business activities, usually from the sale of goods and services to customers. In many countries, such as the United Kingdom, Revenue is referred to as turnover. Some companies receive Revenue from interest, dividends or royalties paid to them by other companies.

Design patent

In the United States, a Design patent is a patent granted on the ornamental design of a functional item. Design patents are a type of industrial design right. Ornamental designs of jewelry, furniture, beverage containers and computer icons are examples of objects that are covered by Design patents.

Plants

Plants are living organisms belonging to the kingdom Plantae. They include familiar organisms such as trees, herbs, bushes, grasses, vines, ferns, mosses, and green algae. The scientific study of plants, known as botany, has identified about 350,000 extant species of plants, defined as seed plants, bryophytes, ferns and fern allies.

Prior probability

In Bayesian statistical inference, a Prior probability distribution of an uncertain quantity p is the probability distribution that would express one`s uncertainty about p before the `data` is taken into account. It is meant to attribute uncertainty rather than randomness to the uncertain quantity. The unknown quantity may be a parameter or latent variable.

Software patents

Software patent does not have a universally accepted definition. One definition suggested by the Foundation for a Free Information Infrastructure is that a software patent is a `patent on any performance of a computer realised by means of a computer program`.

There is intense debate over the extent to which Software patents should be granted, if at all. Important issues concerning Software patents include:

· Where the boundary between patentable and non-patentable software should lie;

· Whether the inventive step and non-obviousness requirement is applied too loosely to software; and

· Whether patents covering software discourage, rather than encourage, innovation.

Trademark

A Trademark is a distinctive sign or indicator used by an individual, business organization, or other legal entity to identify that the products and/or services to consumers with which the Trademark appears originate from a unique source and to distinguish its products or services from those of other entities.

United States

The United States of America (commonly referred to as the United States, the U.S., the United StatesA, or America) is a federal constitutional republic comprising fifty states and a federal district. The country is situated mostly in central North America, where its forty-eight contiguous states and Washington, D.C., the capital district, lie between the Pacific and Atlantic Oceans, bordered by Canada to the north and Mexico to the south. The state of Alaska is in the northwest of the continent, with Canada to its east and Russia to the west across the Bering Strait.

Utility

In economics, Utility is a measure of relative satisfaction. Given this measure, one may speak meaningfully of increasing or decreasing Utility, and thereby explain economic behavior in terms of attempts to increase one`s Utility. Utility is often modeled to be affected by consumption of various goods and services, possession of wealth and spending of leisure time.

Artificial neural network

An Artificial neural network is a mathematical model or computational model that tries to simulate the structure and/or functional aspects of biological neural networks. It consists of an interconnected group of artificial neurons and processes information using a connectionist approach to computation. In most cases an Artificial neural network is an adaptive system that changes its structure based on external or internal information that flows through the network during the learning phase.

Business process

A Business process or business method is a collection of related, structured activities or tasks that produce a specific service or product for a particular customer or customers. It often can be visualized with a flowchart as a sequence of activities.

Overview

There are three types of Business processes:

· Management processes, the processes that govern the operation of a system. Typical management processes include `Corporate Governance` and `Strategic Management`.

· Operational processes, processes that constitute the core business and create the primary value stream. Typical operational processes are Purchasing, Manufacturing, Marketing and Sales.

· Supporting processes, which support the core processes. Examples include Accounting, Recruitment, Technical support.

Camera

A Camera is a device that records images, either as a still photograph or as moving images known as videos or movies. The term comes from the Camera obscura , an early mechanism of projecting images where an entire room functioned as a real-time imaging system; the modern Camera evolved from the Camera obscura.

Cameras may work with the light of the visible spectrum or with other portions of the electromagnetic spectrum.

Trade Secret

A Trade secret is a formula, practice, process, design, instrument, pattern, or compilation of information which is not generally known or reasonably ascertainable, by which a business can obtain an economic advantage over competitors or customers. In some jurisdictions, such secrets are referred to as `confidential information` or `classified information`.

The precise language by which a Trade secret is defined varies by jurisdiction . However, there are three factors that, although subject to differing interpretations, are common to all such definitions: a Trade secret is information that:

· is not generally known to the public;

· confers some sort of economic benefit on its holder (where this benefit must derive specifically from its not being generally known, not just from the value of the information itself);

· is the subject of reasonable efforts to maintain its secrecy

By comparison, under US law, `A Trade secret, as defined under 18 U.S.C. Â§ 1839(3) (A), (B) (1996), has three parts: (1) information; (2) reasonable measures taken to protect the information; and (3) which derives independent economic value from not being publicly known.`

	A company can protect its confidential information through non-compete and non-disclosure contracts with its employees (within the constraints of employment law, including only restraint that is reasonable in geographic and time scope).
Uniform Trade Secrets Act	The Uniform Trade Secrets Act is a model law drafted by the National Conference of Commissioners on Uniform State Laws to better define rights and remedies of common law trade secret. It has been adopted by 46 states, the District of Columbia and the U.S. Virgin Islands. Massachusetts, New Jersey, New York and Texas have not adopted the Uniform Trade Secrets Act. Some of these states continue to apply common law to trade secrets, and some have adopted separate state statutes.
Advanced Micro Devices	Advanced Micro Devices, Inc. is an American multinational semiconductor company based in Sunnyvale, California, that develops computer processors and related technologies for commercial and consumer markets. Its main products include microprocessors, motherboard chipsets, embedded processors and graphics processors for servers, workstations and personal computers, and processor technologies for handheld devices, digital television, automobiles, game consoles, and other embedded systems applications.
Digital Millennium Copyright Act	The Digital Millennium Copyright Act is a United States copyright law that implements two 1996 treaties of the World Intellectual Property Organization (WIPO). It criminalizes production and dissemination of technology, devices, or services intended to circumvent measures (commonly known as digital rights management or DRM) that control access to copyrighted works. It also criminalizes the act of circumventing an access control, whether or not there is actual infringement of copyright itself.
Policy	A Policy is typically described as a principle or rule to guide decisions and achieve rational outcome(s). The term is not normally used to denote what is actually done, this is normally referred to as either procedure or protocol. Whereas a Policy will contain the \`what\` and the \`why\`, procedures or protocols contain the \`what\`, the \`how\`, the \`where\`, and the \`when\`.
Digital Rights Management	Digital rights management is a generic term for access control technologies that can be used by hardware manufacturers, publishers, copyright holders and individuals to impose limitations on the usage of digital content and devices. The term is used to describe any technology that inhibits uses of digital content not desired or intended by the content provider. The term does not generally refer to other forms of copy protection which can be circumvented without modifying the file or device, such as serial numbers or keyfiles.

Sumatriptan	Sumatriptan is a triptan drug including a sulfonamide group for the treatment of migraine headaches. It is marketed and manufactured by GlaxoSmithKline as well as various generic drug manufacturers. Sumatriptan was the first triptan available (in 1991), and, in the United States and most developed countries, is available only by medical prescription.
Firing	\`Firing\` is a common colloquial term in the English language for termination. It is also often known as being \`dismissed\`, \`sacked\` , \`released\`, \`discharged\`, \`canned\`, \`axed\`, \`given walking papers\`, \`let go\`, \`relieved of duty\`, \`boned\`, or \`being given a pink slip\`. Most US states have adopted the at-will employment contract that allows the employer to dismiss employees without having to provide a justified reason f, although the variety of court cases that have come out of \`at-will\` dismissals have made such at-will contracts ambiguous.
Competitiveness	Competitiveness is a comparative concept of the ability and performance of a firm, sub-sector or country to sell and supply goods and/or services in a given market. Although widely used in economics and business management, the usefulness of the concept, particularly in the context of national competitiveness, is vigorously disputed by economists, such as Paul Krugman . The term may also be applied to markets, where it is used to refer to the extent to which the market structure may be regarded as perfectly competitive.
Dominant design	Dominant Design is a Technology Management concept identifying key technological designs that become a de-facto standard in their market place. When a new technology emerges (e.g. computer GUI operating systems) - often firms will introduce a number of alternative designs (e.g. Microsoft - Windows, Apple Inc. - Mac OS and IBM - OS2) .
Technology Development	Technological development is the process of research and development of technology. Many emerging technologies are expected to become generally applied in the near future. The new Technology development process leans on the New product development process. It starts with a new technological idea, via research and development through to the use of a technology (e.g. by introducing products that are based on the new technology in market).

Resources	A resource is any physical or virtual entity of limited availability, or anything used to help one earn a living. In most cases, commercial or even ethic factors require resource allocation through resource management. As resources are very useful, we attach some information value to them.
Gate oxide	The Gate oxide is the third region of the MOSFET between the source and drain. It is a thin layer of pure, defect free, 5 - 200 nm thick thermally grown oxide. It serves as the dielectric layer so that the gate can sustain as high as 1 to 5 MV/cm transverse electric field in order to strongly modulate the conductance of the channel.
Kilobit	A Kilobit is an expression of grouped bits meaning 1,000 (10^3) bits. Use of the term to denote a kibibit, although the most common use due to the nature of bits (binary digits), is deprecated and contrary to international standard. The term \`Kilobit\` is most commonly used in the expression of data rates (digital communication speeds) in the abbreviated form \`kbps\`, \`kb/s\`, or \`kbit/s\`, meaning \`Kilobits per second\`.
Shift registers	In digital circuits, a shift register is a cascade of flip flops, sharing the same clock, which has the output of any one but the last flip-flop connected to the \`data\` input of the next one in the chain, resulting in a circuit that shifts by one position the one-dimensional \`bit array\` stored in it, shifting in the data present at its input and shifting out the last bit in the array, when enabled to do so by a transition of the clock input. More generally, a shift register may be multidimensional, such that its \`data in\` input and stage outputs are themselves bit arrays: this is implemented simply by running several Shift registers of the same bit-length in parallel. Shift registers can have both parallel and serial inputs and outputs.
Competitive advantage	Competitive advantage is a position of a company in a competitive landscape that allows the company earning return on investments higher than the cost of investments. Competitive advantage should be relevant, unique, and sustainable. Competitive advantage is a theory that seeks to address some of the criticisms of comparative advantage.

Disaster	A Disaster is the tragedy of a natural or human-made hazard (a hazard is a situation which poses a level of threat to life, health, property) that negatively affects society or environment. In contemporary academia, Disasters are seen as the consequence of inappropriately managed risk. These risks are the product of hazards and vulnerability.
Denial	· Closed circle · Cognitive dissonance · Disagreement · Dismissiveness · Hostility · Lie · Non-denial denial · Non-apology apology · Psychological manipulation · Polite fiction · Self-deception · Self-fulfilling prophecy · The closet .

Xerox	Xerox Corporation is a global document management company which manufactures and sells a range of color and black-and-white printers, multifunction systems, photo copiers, digital production printing presses, and related consulting services and supplies. Xerox is headquartered in Norwalk, Connecticut , though its largest population of employees is based in and around Rochester, New York, the area in which the company was founded. The Xerox 914 was the first one-piece plain paper photocopier, and sold in the thousands. Xerox was founded in 1906 in Rochester, New York as \`The Haloid Company\`, which originally manufactured photographic paper and equipment.
Strategic planning	Strategic planning is an organization\`s process of defining its strategy, or direction, and making decisions on allocating its resources to pursue this strategy, including its capital and people. Various business analysis techniques can be used in Strategic planning, including SWOT analysis (Strengths, Weaknesses, Opportunities, and Threats), PEST analysis (Political, Economic, Social, and Technological), STEER analysis (Socio-cultural, Technological, Economic, Ecological, and Regulatory factors), and EPISTEL . Strategic planning is the formal consideration of an organization\`s future course. All Strategic planning deals with at least one of three key questions:  · \`What do we do?\`  · \`For whom do we do it?\`  · \`How do we excel?\` In business Strategic planning, the third question is better phrased \`How can we beat or avoid competition?\`.
Case study	A Case study is one of several ways of doing research whether it is social science related or even socially related. It is an intensive study of a single group, incident, or community. Other ways include experiments, surveys, or analysis of archival information.
Constraint	In mathematics, a constraint is a condition that a solution to an optimization problem must satisfy. There are two types of constraints: equality constraints and inequality constraints. The set of solutions that satisfy all constraints is called the feasible set.

Chapter 5. STRATEGIC ACTION

Benchmarking	Benchmarking is the process of comparing one`s business processes and performance metrics to industry bests and/or best practices from other industries. Dimensions typically measured are quality, time, and cost. Improvements from learning mean doing things better, faster, and cheaper.
Competitive advantage	Competitive advantage is a position of a company in a competitive landscape that allows the company earning return on investments higher than the cost of investments. Competitive advantage should be relevant, unique, and sustainable.
	Competitive advantage is a theory that seeks to address some of the criticisms of comparative advantage.
Collaboration	Collaboration is a recursive process where two or more people or organizations work together in an intersection of common goals -- for example, an intellectual endeavor that is creative in nature--by sharing knowledge, learning and building consensus. Most Collaboration requires leadership, although the form of leadership can be social within a decentralized and egalitarian group. In particular, teams that work collaboratively can obtain greater resources, recognition and reward when facing competition for finite resources.
Nominative determinism	Nominative determinism refers to the theory that a person`s name is given an influential role in reflecting key attributes of his job, profession, but real examples are more highly prized, the more obscure the better.
Venture capital	Venture capital is provided as seed funding to early-stage, high-potential, growth companies and more often after the seed funding round as growth funding round (also referred as series A round) in the interest of generating a return through an eventual realization event such as an IPO or trade sale of the company. To put it simply, an investment firm will give money to a growing company. The growing company will then use this money to advertise, do research, build infrastructure, develop products etc.
Decentralization	Delegation is a more extensive form of Decentralization. Through delegation central governments transfer responsibility for decision-making and administration of public functions to semi-autonomous organizations not wholly controlled by the central government, but ultimately accountable to it. Governments delegate responsibilities when they create public enterprises or corporations, housing authorities, transportation authorities, special service districts, semi-autonomous school districts, regional development corporations, or special project implementation units.

Chapter 5. STRATEGIC ACTION

Strategic business unit	Strategic business unit is understood as a business unit within the overall corporate identity which is distinguishable from other business because it serves a defined external market where management can conduct strategic planning in relation to products and markets. The unique small business unit benefits that a firm aggressively promotes in a consistent manner. When companies become really large, they are best thought of as being composed of a number of businesses (or Strategic business units).
Core competency	A Core competency is a specific factor that a business sees as being central to the way it, or its employees, works. It fulfills three key criteria: · It provides consumer benefits · It is not easy for competitors to imitate · It can be leveraged widely to many products and markets A Core competency can take various forms, including technical/subject matter know-how, a reliable process and/or close relationships with customers and suppliers. It may also include product development or culture, such as employee dedication. Core competencies are particular strengths relative to other organizations in the industry which provide the fundamental basis for the provision of added value.
Synthetic environment	Synthetic environment refers to simulations on the internet that represent activities at a high level of realism, from simulations of theaters of war to factories and manufacturing processes. These environments may be created within a single computer or a vast distributed network connected by local and wide area networks and augmented by super-realistic special effects and accurate behavioral models. Synthetic environment allows visualization of and immersion into the environment being simulated. The Synthetic environment could be divided into the terms below to eliminate ambiguity and confusion: · Synthetic natural environment - Representation of climate, weather, terrain, oceans, space, etc. · Synthetic human-made environment - Representation of human-made structures like buildings, bridges, and roads

· Synthetic psychological environment - Representation of psychological influences on individuals and/or groups based on demography and other cultural factors.

Gold Star

The Gold Star medal is a special insignia that identifies recipients of the title `Hero` in the Soviet Union and several post-Soviet states.

The Gold Star was established by the decree of the Presidium of the Supreme Soviet on August 1, 1939. Previously, Heroes of the Soviet Union were awarded the Order of Lenin and a special diploma (gramota, Ð³Ñ€Ð°Ð¼Ð¾Ñ‚Ð°) describing the heroic feat. The medal was introduced to distinguish these heroes from other Order of Lenin recipients.

Communications management

Communications management is the systematic planning, implementing, monitoring, and revision of all the channels of communication within an organization, and between organizations; it also includes the organization and dissemination of new communication directives connected with an organization, network, designing internal and external communications directives, and managing the flow of information, including online communication. New technology forces constant innovation on the part of communications managers.

Management Consulting

Management consulting indicates both the industry of, and the practice of, helping organizations improve their performance, primarily through the analysis of existing business problems and development of plans for improvement.

Organizations hire the services of management consultants for a number of reasons, including gaining external (and presumably objective) advice and access to the consultants` specialized expertise.

Because of their exposure to and relationships with numerous organizations, consulting firms are also said to be aware of industry `best practices`, although the transferability of such practices from one organization to another may be limited or problematic.

Business process

A Business process or business method is a collection of related, structured activities or tasks that produce a specific service or product for a particular customer or customers. It often can be visualized with a flowchart as a sequence of activities.

Overview

There are three types of Business processes:

· Management processes, the processes that govern the operation of a system. Typical management processes include `Corporate Governance` and `Strategic Management`.

· Operational processes, processes that constitute the core business and create the primary value stream. Typical operational processes are Purchasing, Manufacturing, Marketing and Sales.

· Supporting processes, which support the core processes. Examples include Accounting, Recruitment, Technical support.

Group

In business, a group, business group, corporate group) alliance is most commonly a legal entity that is a type of conglomerate or holding company consisting of a parent company and subsidiaries. Typical examples are Adidas group or Icelandair group.
In United Arab Emirates, Business group can also be knows as Trade association.

Outsourcing

Outsourcing often refers to the process of contracting to a third-party. While Outsourcing may be viewed as a component to the growing division of labor encompassing all societies, the term did not enter the English-speaking lexicon until the 1980s. Since the 1980s, transnational corporations have increased subcontracting across national boundaries.

Procter ' Gamble

Procter is a surname, and may also refer to:

· Bryan Waller Procter (pseud. Barry Cornwall), English poet

· Goodwin Procter, American law firm

· Procter ' Gamble, consumer products multinational `

Global Delivery Model

The term Global delivery model is typically associated with companies engaged in IT consulting and services delivery business and using a model of executing a technology project using a team that is distributed globally. While the commonly understood meaning of the term implies globally distributed resources, the term itself has acquired a broader definition. Gartner, for example, defines Global delivery model to encompass a `focus on the technical skills, process rigor, tools, methodologies, overall structure and strategies for seamlessly delivering IT-enabled services from global locations.`

Software Engineering	Software engineering is a profession and field of study dedicated to designing, implementing, and modifying software so that it is of higher quality, more affordable, maintainable, and faster to build. The term Software engineering first appeared in the 1968 NATO Software engineering Conference, and was meant to provoke thought regarding the perceived `software crisis` at the time. Since the field is still relatively young compared to its sister fields of engineering, there is still much debate around what Software engineering actually is, and if it conforms to the classical definition of engineering.
Time to market	In commerce, Time to market is the length of time it takes from a product being conceived until its being available for sale. Time to market is important in industries where products are outmoded quickly. A common assumption is that Time to market matters most for first-of-a-kind products, but actually the leader often has the luxury of time, while the clock is clearly running for the followers.
Audit	The general definition of an Audit is an evaluation of a person, organization, system, process, enterprise, project or product. The term most commonly refers to Audits in accounting, but similar concepts also exist in project management, quality management, and for energy conservation. Audits are performed to ascertain the validity and reliability of information; also to provide an assessment of a system`s internal control. The goal of an Audit is to express an opinion on the person / organization / system (etc) in question, under evaluation based on work done on a test basis. Due to practical constraints, an Audit seeks to provide only reasonable assurance that the statements are free from material error. Hence, statistical sampling is often adopted in Audits. In the case of financial Audits, a set of financial statements are said to be true and fair when they are free of material misstatements - a concept influenced by both quantitative and qualitative factors.
Software Testing	Software testing is an investigation conducted to provide stakeholders with information about the quality of the product or service under test. Software testing also provides an objective, independent view of the software to allow the business to appreciate and understand the risks at implementation of the software. Test techniques include, but are not limited to, the process of executing a program or application with the intent of finding software bugs. Software testing can also be stated as the process of validating and verifying that a software program/application/product: · meets the business and technical requirements that guided its design and development;

· works as expected; and

· can be implemented with the same characteristics
Software testing, depending on the testing method employed, can be implemented at any time in the development process.

Suit	A suit is a set of garments crafted from the same cloth, consisting of at least a jacket and trousers. Lounge suits are the most common style of Western suit, originating in England as country wear. Other types of suit still worn today are firstly the dinner suit, part of black tie, which arose as a lounging alternative to dress coats in much the same way as the day lounge suit came to replace frock and morning coats; and secondly, rarely worn today, the morning suit.
Time Warner	Time Warner Inc. (NYSE: Time Warner X) is the world`s third largest media and entertainment conglomerate by market capitalization (behind News Corporation, headquartered in the Time Warner Center in New York City. (TimeWarner.com Fact Sheet Page) Formerly three separate companies (and owns the assets of a fourth, Turner Broadcasting System, Inc., acquired by a pre-AOL merger Time Warner in 1996): Warner Communications, Inc.
Volvo	The Volvo Group is a Swedish supplier of commercial vehicles such as trucks, buses and construction equipment, drive systems for marine and industrial applications, aerospace components and financial services. Although Volvo was incorporated in 1915 as a subsidiary of AB SKF, a Swedish ball bearing manufacturer, the auto manufacturer was officially founded on 14 April 1927, when the first car rolled out of the factory in Hisingen, Gothenburg. Volvo means `I roll` in Latin, conjugated from `volvere` .
Leadership	In response to the criticism of the trait approach, theorists began to research Leadership as a set of behaviors, evaluating the behavior of `successful` leaders, determining a behavior taxonomy and identifying broad Leadership styles. David McClelland, for example, saw Leadership skills, not so much as a set of traits, but as a pattern of motives. He claimed that successful leaders will tend to have a high need for power, a low need for affiliation, and a high level of what he called activity inhibition (one might call it self-control).
Market development	A Market development strategy targets non-buying customers in currently targeted segments. It also targets new customers in new segments.

	A marketing manager has to think about the following questions before implementing a Market development strategy: Is it profitable? Will it require the introduction of new or modified products? Is the customer and channel well enough researched and understood? The marketing manager uses these four groups to give more focus to the market segment decision: existing customers, competitor customers, non-buying in current segments, new segments.
Advanced Micro Devices	Advanced Micro Devices, Inc. is an American multinational semiconductor company based in Sunnyvale, California, that develops computer processors and related technologies for commercial and consumer markets. Its main products include microprocessors, motherboard chipsets, embedded processors and graphics processors for servers, workstations and personal computers, and processor technologies for handheld devices, digital television, automobiles, game consoles, and other embedded systems applications.
Intellectual property	Intellectual property is a term referring to a number of distinct types of creations of the mind for which property rights are recognised--and the corresponding fields of law. Under Intellectual property law, owners are granted certain exclusive rights to a variety of intangible assets, such as musical, literary, and artistic works; discoveries and inventions; and words, phrases, symbols, and designs. Common types of Intellectual property include copyrights, trademarks, patents, industrial design rights and trade secrets in some jurisdictions.
Competition	Co-operative Competition is based upon promoting mutual survival - \`everyone wins\`. Adam Smith\`s \`invisible hand\` is a process where individuals compete to improve their level of happiness but compete in a cooperative manner through peaceful exchange and without violating other people. Cooperative Competition focuses individuals/groups/organisms against the environment.
Resource allocation	Resource allocation is used to assign the available resources in an economic way. It is part of resource management. In project management, Resource allocation is the scheduling of activities and the resources required by those activities while taking into consideration both the resource availability and the project time.
Strategic leadership	Strategic Leadership provides the vision and direction for the growth and success of an organization. To successfully deal with change, all executives need the skills and tools for both strategy formulation and implementation. Managing change and ambiguity requires strategic leaders who not only provide a sense of direction, but who can also build ownership and alignment within their workgroups to implement change.

Chapter 5. STRATEGIC ACTION

Adaptive system	The term adaptation arises mainly in the biological scope as a trial to study the relationship between the characteristics (anatomic structure, physiological processes or behavior) of living beings and their environments. Currently, in biology, the term adaptation has a clear and concise meaning: a biological adaptation is an anatomic structure, a physiological process or a behavior`s trait of an organism that has been selected by the natural evolution in such a way that this characteristic increase the probability of reproduction of an organism. An Adaptive system is a set of interacting or interdependent entities, real or abstract, forming an integrated whole that together are able to respond to environmental changes or changes in the interacting parts.
Camera	A Camera is a device that records images, either as a still photograph or as moving images known as videos or movies. The term comes from the Camera obscura , an early mechanism of projecting images where an entire room functioned as a real-time imaging system; the modern Camera evolved from the Camera obscura. Cameras may work with the light of the visible spectrum or with other portions of the electromagnetic spectrum.
Asset	In financial accounting, Assets are economic resources. Anything tangible or intangible that is capable of being owned or controlled to produce value and that is held to have positive economic value is considered an Asset. Simplistically stated, Assets represent ownership of value that can be converted into cash (although cash itself is also considered an Asset).
Asset management	Asset management is a term used in various contexts. The primary ones are listed below: 1. Financial asset management is used extensively in financial services industries in relation to the cost/risk/returns associated with different financial products. This may also include the financial or accountancy view of certain physical assets 2. Physical asset management deals with the optimal whole life cycle management of physical assets and infrastructure and is a rapidly growing discipline in many industry sectors 3. The term Enterprise asset management tends to be oriented more towards the usage of informations systems in support of physical asset management.

Mergers and acquisitions

The phrase Mergers and acquisitions refers to the aspect of corporate strategy, corporate finance and management dealing with the buying, selling and combining of different companies that can aid, finance, or help a growing company in a given industry grow rapidly without having to create another business entity.

An acquisition, also known as a takeover or a buyout, is the buying of one company (the `target`) by another. Merger is when two companies combine together to form a new company alltogether.

TD Waterhouse

TD Waterhouse is the brand used for both British and Canadian brokerages within the TD Bank Financial Group. It was also formerly used for TD`s American brokerage.

TD`s original brokerage was from the purchase of Gardiner Group Stockbrokers, which was renamed Greenline.

Brown

Brown is a color term, denoting a range of composite colors produced by a mixture of orange, red or yellow with black. The term is from Old English brún, in origin for any dusky or dark shade of color. The Common Germanic adjective *brûnoz, *brûnâ meant both dark colors and a glistening or shining quality, whence burnish.

Team

A team comprises a group of people or animals linked in a common purpose. teams are especially appropriate for conducting tasks that are high in complexity and have many interdependent subtasks.
A group in itself does not necessarily constitute a team.

Basic indicator approach

Basic indicator approach is a set of operational risk measurement techniques proposed under Basel II capital adequacy rules for banking institutions.

Basel II requires all banking institutions to set aside capital for operational risk. Basic indicator approach is much simpler compared to the alternative approaches (i.e. standardized approach (operational risk) and advanced measurement approach) and this has been recommended for banks without significant international operations.

Goal

A Goal or objective is a projected state of affairs that a person or a system plans or intends to achieve--a personal or organizational desired end-point in some sort of assumed development. Many people endeavor to reach Goals within a finite time by setting deadlines.
A desire or an intention becomes a Goal if and only if one activates an action for achieving it .

Market dominance	Market dominance is a measure of the strength of a brand, product, service, relative to competitive offerings. There is often a geographic element to the competitive landscape. In defining Market dominance, you must see to what extent a product, brand, or firm controls a product category in a given geographic area.
Innovation	Innovation is a change in the thought process for doing something or `new stuff that is made useful`. It may refer to an incremental emergent or radical and revolutionary changes in thinking, products, processes, or organizations. Following Schumpeter (1934), contributors to the scholarly literature on Innovation typically distinguish between invention, an idea made manifest, and Innovation, ideas applied successfully in practice.
File sharing	File sharing is the practice of distributing or providing access to digitally stored information, such as computer programs, multi-media (audio, video), documents, transmission, and distribution models. Common methods are manual sharing using removable media, centralized computer file server installations on computer networks, World Wide Web-based hyperlinked documents, and the use of distributed peer-to-peer (P2P) networking.
Enterprise manufacturing intelligence	Enterprise manufacturing intelligence is a term which applies to software used to bring a corporation`s manufacturing-related data together from many sources for the purposes of reporting, analysis, visual summaries, and passing data between enterprise-level and plant-floor systems. As data is combined from multiple sources, it can be given a new structure or context that will help users find what they need regardless of where it came from. The primary goal is to turn large amounts of manufacturing data into real knowledge and drive business results based on that knowledge.
Strategic management	Strategic management is the conduct of drafting, implementing and evaluating cross-functional decisions that will enable an organization to achieve its long-term objectives. It is the process of specifying the organization`s mission, vision and objectives, developing policies and plans, often in terms of projects and programs, which are designed to achieve these objectives, and then allocating resources to implement the policies and plans, projects and programs. A balanced scorecard is often used to evaluate the overall performance of the business and its progress towards objectives.
Enterprise resource planning	Enterprise resource planning is an Integrated computer-based system used to manage internal and external resources, including tangible assets, financial resources, materials, and human resources. It is a software architecture whose purpose is to facilitate the flow of information between all business functions inside the boundaries of the organization and manage the connections to outside stakeholders. Built on a centralized database and normally utilizing a common computing platform, Enterprise resource planning systems consolidate all business operations into a uniform and enterprise-wide system environment.

Research and development	The phrase Research and development according to the Organization for Economic Co-operation and Development, refers to `creative work undertaken on a systematic basis in order to increase the stock of knowledge, including knowledge of man, culture and society, and the use of this stock of knowledge to devise new applications`. New product design and development is more often than not a crucial factor in the survival of a company. In an industry that is fast changing, firms must continually revise their design and range of products.
Venture management	Venture Management is an emerging business management discipline. This discipline is focused on the skills and practices required to manage the rapid growth of new business in highly dynamic environments. These environments are often characterized by rapid technology change.
Gene	A Gene is the basic unit of heredity in a living organism. All living things depend on Genes. Genes hold the information to build and maintain their cells and pass Genetic traits to offspring.
Operational definition	An Operational definition is a demonstration of a process - such as a variable, term, or object - in terms of the specific process or set of validation tests used to determine its presence and quantity. The term was coined by Percy Williams Bridgman . Properties described in this manner must be sufficiently accessible, so that persons other than the definer may independently measure or test for them at will.
Vertical integration	In microeconomics and management, the term Vertical integration describes a style of management control. Vertically integrated companies in a supply chain are united through a common owner. Usually each member of the supply chain produces a different product or (market-specific) service, and the products combine to satisfy a common need.

Research and development

The phrase Research and development according to the Organization for Economic Co-operation and Development, refers to `creative work undertaken on a systematic basis in order to increase the stock of knowledge, including knowledge of man, culture and society, and the use of this stock of knowledge to devise new applications`.

New product design and development is more often than not a crucial factor in the survival of a company. In an industry that is fast changing, firms must continually revise their design and range of products.

Vertical integration

In microeconomics and management, the term Vertical integration describes a style of management control. Vertically integrated companies in a supply chain are united through a common owner. Usually each member of the supply chain produces a different product or (market-specific) service, and the products combine to satisfy a common need.

Innovation

Innovation is a change in the thought process for doing something or `new stuff that is made useful`. It may refer to an incremental emergent or radical and revolutionary changes in thinking, products, processes, or organizations. Following Schumpeter (1934), contributors to the scholarly literature on Innovation typically distinguish between invention, an idea made manifest, and Innovation, ideas applied successfully in practice.

Economic value

The Economic value of a good or service has puzzled economists since the beginning of the discipline. First, economists tried to estimate the value of a good to an individual alone, and extend that definition to goods which can be exchanged. From this analysis came the concepts value in use and value in exchange.Wealth maximization predicts that a person will choose to obtain the good or service in the place where it is cheapest, where the amount given up is the least.Value is linked to price through the mechanism of exchange. When an economist observes an exchange, two important value functions are revealed: those of the buyer and seller. Just as the buyer reveals what he is willing to pay for a certain amount of a good, so too does the seller reveal what it costs him to give up the good.

Value chain

The Value chain is a concept from business management that was first described and popularized by Michael Porter in his 1985 best-seller, Competitive Advantage: Creating and Sustaining Superior Performance.

A Value chain is a chain of activities for a firm operating in a specific industry. The business unit is the appropriate level for construction of a Value chain, not the divisional level or corporate level.

Xerox	Xerox Corporation is a global document management company which manufactures and sells a range of color and black-and-white printers, multifunction systems, photo copiers, digital production printing presses, and related consulting services and supplies. Xerox is headquartered in Norwalk, Connecticut , though its largest population of employees is based in and around Rochester, New York, the area in which the company was founded. The Xerox 914 was the first one-piece plain paper photocopier, and sold in the thousands. Xerox was founded in 1906 in Rochester, New York as \`The Haloid Company\`, which originally manufactured photographic paper and equipment.
Nominative determinism	Nominative determinism refers to the theory that a person\`s name is given an influential role in reflecting key attributes of his job, profession, but real examples are more highly prized, the more obscure the better.
Six Sigma	Six Sigma is a business management strategy originally developed by Motorola, USA in 1981. As of 2010, it enjoys widespread application in many sectors of industry, although its application is not without controversy. Six Sigma seeks to improve the quality of process outputs by identifying and removing the causes of defects (errors) and minimizing variability in manufacturing and business processes. It uses a set of quality management methods, including statistical methods, and creates a special infrastructure of people within the organization (\`Black Belts\`, \`Green Belts\`, etc).
Star	A Star is a massive, luminous ball of plasma held together by gravity. The nearest Star to Earth is the Sun, which is the source of most of the energy on Earth. Other Stars are visible in the night sky, when they are not outshone by the Sun.
Hostile work environment	A Hostile work environment exists when an employee experiences workplace harassment and fears going to work because of the offensive, intimidating, religion, sex, national origin, age, disability, veteran status, or, in some jurisdictions, sexual orientation, political affiliation, citizenship status, marital status, or personal appearance. Hostile work environment is also one of the two legal categories of sexual harassment. A Hostile work environment may also be defined as when a boss or manager begins to engage in a manner designed to make you quit in retaliation for your actions.
Cross-functional team	A cross-functional team is a group of employees from various functional areas of the organization - research, engineering, marketing, finance, human resources, and operations, for example - who are all focused on a specific objective and are responsible to work as a team to improve coordination and innovation across divisions and resolve mutual problems.

Demand	In economics, Demand is the desire to own anything and the ability to pay for it and willigness to pay . The term Demand signifies the ability or the willingness to buy a particular commodity at a given point of time. Demand is also defined elsewhere as a measure of preferences that is weighted by income.
Venture capital	Venture capital is provided as seed funding to early-stage, high-potential, growth companies and more often after the seed funding round as growth funding round (also referred as series A round) in the interest of generating a return through an eventual realization event such as an IPO or trade sale of the company. To put it simply, an investment firm will give money to a growing company. The growing company will then use this money to advertise, do research, build infrastructure, develop products etc.
Technology transfer	Technology transfer is the process of sharing of skills, knowledge, technologies, methods of manufacturing, samples of manufacturing and facilities among governments and other institutions to ensure that scientific and technological developments are accessible to a wider range of users who can then further develop and exploit the technology into new products, processes, applications, materials or services. It is closely related to (and may arguably be considered a subset of) knowledge transfer. Technology brokers are people who discovered how to bridge the disparate worlds and apply scientific concepts or processes to new situations or circumstances.
Case study	A Case study is one of several ways of doing research whether it is social science related or even socially related. It is an intensive study of a single group, incident, or community. Other ways include experiments, surveys, or analysis of archival information.
Concepts	Kant declared that human minds possess pure or a priori concepts. Instead of being abstracted from individual perceptions, like empirical concepts, they originate in the mind itself. He called these concepts categories, in the sense of the word that means predicate, attribute, characteristic, or quality.
Germanium	Germanium is a chemical element with the symbol Ge and atomic number 32. It is a lustrous, hard, grayish-white metalloid in the carbon group, chemically similar to its group neighbors tin and silicon. Germanium has five naturally occurring isotopes ranging in atomic mass number from 70 to 76. It forms a large number of organometallic compounds, including tetraethylgermane and isobutylgermane. Because few minerals contain it in large concentration, Germanium was discovered comparatively late despite the fact that it is relatively abundant in the Earth`s crust.

Prior probability	In Bayesian statistical inference, a Prior probability distribution of an uncertain quantity p is the probability distribution that would express one`s uncertainty about p before the `data` is taken into account. It is meant to attribute uncertainty rather than randomness to the uncertain quantity. The unknown quantity may be a parameter or latent variable.
Path dependence	Path dependence explains how the set of decisions one faces for any given circumstance is limited by the decisions one has made in the past, even though past circumstances may no longer be relevant. In economics and the social sciences the phrase implies either: · (A) that `history matters` - a broad concept, or · (B) that predictable amplifications of small differences are a disproportionate cause of later circumstances. And, in the `strong` form, that this historical hang-over is inefficient. The first usage, (A): `history matters` is trivially true in the explanatory context; everything has causes. And, in these fields, the direct influence of earlier states isn`t notable (compare `path dependent` options in finance, where the influence of history can be non standard).
Western Electric Company	Western Electric Company was an American electrical engineering company, the manufacturing arm of AT'T from 1881 to 1995. It was the scene of a number of technological innovations and also some seminal developments in industrial management. It also served as the purchasing agent for the member companies of the Bell System.
Market	A Market is any one of a variety of different systems, institutions, procedures, social relations and infrastructures whereby persons trade, and goods and services are exchanged, forming part of the economy. It is an arrangement that allows buyers and sellers to exchange things. Markets vary in size, range, geographic scale, location, types and variety of human communities, as well as the types of goods and services traded.
Competitive advantage	Competitive advantage is a position of a company in a competitive landscape that allows the company earning return on investments higher than the cost of investments. Competitive advantage should be relevant, unique, and sustainable.

	Competitive advantage is a theory that seeks to address some of the criticisms of comparative advantage.
File sharing	File sharing is the practice of distributing or providing access to digitally stored information, such as computer programs, multi-media (audio, video), documents, transmission, and distribution models. Common methods are manual sharing using removable media, centralized computer file server installations on computer networks, World Wide Web-based hyperlinked documents, and the use of distributed peer-to-peer (P2P) networking.
Evaluation	Evaluation is systematic determination of merit, worth, and significance of something or someone using criteria against a set of standards. Evaluation often is used to characterize and appraise subjects of interest in a wide range of human enterprises, including the arts, criminal justice, foundations and non-profit organizations, government, health care, and other human services.
Mergers and acquisitions	The phrase Mergers and acquisitions refers to the aspect of corporate strategy, corporate finance and management dealing with the buying, selling and combining of different companies that can aid, finance, or help a growing company in a given industry grow rapidly without having to create another business entity. An acquisition, also known as a takeover or a buyout, is the buying of one company (the `target`) by another. Merger is when two companies combine together to form a new company alltogether.
Employee retention	Employee retention is a business management term referring to efforts by employers to retain current employees in their workforce. The purpose is to avoid employee turnover and associated costs: hiring and training expenses; productivity loss; lost customers; diminished business; and damaged morale among remaining members of the workforce. Retention is particularly a problem in high stress occupations such as teaching, nursing and social carework.
Rate of return	In finance, Rate of return also known as return on investment (ROI), rate of profit or sometimes just return, is the ratio of money gained or lost (whether realized or unrealized) on an investment relative to the amount of money invested. The amount of money gained or lost may be referred to as interest, profit/loss, gain/loss, or net income/loss. The money invested may be referred to as the asset, capital, principal, or the cost basis of the investment.

Vesting	In law, Vesting is to give an immediately secured right of present or future enjoyment. One has a vested right to an asset that cannot be taken away by any third party, even though one may not yet possess the asset. When the right, interest or title to the present or future possession of a legal estate can be transferred to any other party, it is termed a vested interest.
Communications management	Communications management is the systematic planning, implementing, monitoring, and revision of all the channels of communication within an organization, and between organizations; it also includes the organization and dissemination of new communication directives connected with an organization, network, designing internal and external communications directives, and managing the flow of information, including online communication. New technology forces constant innovation on the part of communications managers.
Product life cycle	Product life cycle Management is the succession of strategies used by management as a product goes through its Product life cycle. The conditions in which a product is sold changes over time and must be managed as it moves through its succession of stages. The Product life cycle goes through many phases, involves many professional disciplines, and requires many skills, tools and processes.
Planning	Planning in organizations and public policy is both the organizational process of creating and maintaining a plan; and the psychological process of thinking about the activities required to create a desired goal on some scale. As such, it is a fundamental property of intelligent behavior. This thought process is essential to the creation and refinement of a plan, or integration of it with other plans, that is, it combines forecasting of developments with the preparation of scenarios of how to react to them.
Forecasting	Forecasting is the process of estimation in unknown situations. Prediction is a similar, but more general term. Both can refer to estimation of time series, cross-sectional or longitudinal data.
Group	In business, a group, business group, corporate group) alliance is most commonly a legal entity that is a type of conglomerate or holding company consisting of a parent company and subsidiaries. Typical examples are Adidas group or Icelandair group. In United Arab Emirates, Business group can also be knows as Trade association.
Enabling	Enabling is a term with a double meaning.

As a positive term, it references patterns of interaction which allow individuals to develop and grow. These may be on any scale, for example within the family, or in wider society as `Enabling acts` designed to empower some group, or create a new authority for a (usually governmental) body.

Generalized additive model	In statistics, the Generalized additive model is a statistical model developed by Trevor Hastie and Rob Tibshirani for blending properties of generalized linear models with additive models. The model specifies a distribution (such as a normal distribution, or a binomial distribution) and a link function g relating the expected value of the distribution to the predictors, and attempts to fit functions f_i to satisfy: $g(\mathrm{E}(Y)) = \beta_0 + f_1(x_1) + f_2(x_2) + \cdots + f_m(x_m).$ The functions $f_i(x_i)$ may be fit using parametric or non-parametric means, thus providing the potential for better fits to data than other methods. The method hence is very general - a typical Generalized additive model might use a scatterplot smoothing function such as a locally weighted mean for $f_1(x_1)$, and then use a factor model for $f_2(x_2)$. By allowing nonparametric fits, well designed Generalized additive models allow good fits to the training data with relaxed assumptions on the actual relationship, perhaps at the expense of interpretability of results.
Concepts	Kant declared that human minds possess pure or a priori concepts. Instead of being abstracted from individual perceptions, like empirical concepts, they originate in the mind itself. He called these concepts categories, in the sense of the word that means predicate, attribute, characteristic, or quality.
Group	In business, a group, business group, corporate group) alliance is most commonly a legal entity that is a type of conglomerate or holding company consisting of a parent company and subsidiaries. Typical examples are Adidas group or Icelandair group. In United Arab Emirates, Business group can also be knows as Trade association.
Case study	A Case study is one of several ways of doing research whether it is social science related or even socially related. It is an intensive study of a single group, incident, or community. Other ways include experiments, surveys, or analysis of archival information.

Idea generation

In business and engineering, new product development is the term used to describe the complete process of bringing a new product or service to market. There are two parallel paths involved in the NPD process: one involves the Idea Generation, product design and detail engineering; the other involves market research and marketing analysis. Companies typically see new product development as the first stage in generating and commercializing new products within the overall strategic process of product life cycle management used to maintain or grow their market share.

· Idea Generation is often called the `fuzzy front end` of the NPD process

· Ideas for new products can be obtained from basic research using a SWOT analysis (Strengths, Weaknesses, Opportunities ' Threats), Market and consumer trends, company`s R'D department, competitors, focus groups, employees, salespeople, corporate spies, trade shows, or Ethnographic discovery methods (searching for user patterns and habits) may also be used to get an insight into new product lines or product features.

· Idea Generation or Brainstorming of new product, service, or store concepts - Idea Generation techniques can begin when you have done your OPPORTUNITY ANALYSIS to support your ideas in the Idea Screening Phase (shown in the next development step).

· Idea Screening

· The object is to eliminate unsound concepts prior to devoting resources to them.

· The screeners should ask several questions:

· Will the customer in the target market benefit from the product?

· What is the size and growth forecasts of the market segment/target market?

· What is the current or expected competitive pressure for the product idea?

· What are the industry sales and market trends the product idea is based on?

· Is it technically feasible to manufacture the product?

· Will the product be profitable when manufactured and delivered to the customer at the target price?

· Concept Development and Testing

· Develop the marketing and engineering details

· Investigate intellectual property issues and search patent data bases

· Who is the target market and who is the decision maker in the purchasing process?

· What product features must the product incorporate?

· What benefits will the product provide?

· How will consumers react to the product?

· How will the product be produced most cost effectively?

· Prove feasibility through virtual computer aided rendering, and rapid prototyping

· What will it cost to produce it?

· Testing the Concept by asking a sample of prospective customers what they think of the idea.

Resources

A resource is any physical or virtual entity of limited availability, or anything used to help one earn a living. In most cases, commercial or even ethic factors require resource allocation through resource management.

As resources are very useful, we attach some information value to them.

Professional

A professional is a member of a vocation founded upon specialised educational training. The word professional traditionally means a person who has obtained a degree in a professional field. The term professional is used more generally to denote a white collar working person, or a person who performs commercially in a field typically reserved for hobbyists or amateurs.

Procter ' Gamble

Procter is a surname, and may also refer to:

· Bryan Waller Procter (pseud. Barry Cornwall), English poet

· Goodwin Procter, American law firm

· Procter ' Gamble, consumer products multinational `

Innovation

Innovation is a change in the thought process for doing something or `new stuff that is made useful`. It may refer to an incremental emergent or radical and revolutionary changes in thinking, products, processes, or organizations. Following Schumpeter (1934), contributors to the scholarly literature on Innovation typically distinguish between invention, an idea made manifest, and Innovation, ideas applied successfully in practice.

Endowment effect

In behavioral economics, the Endowment effect is a hypothesis that people value a good or service more once their property right to it has been established. In other words, people place a higher value on objects they own than objects that they do not. In one experiment, people demanded a higher price for a coffee mug that had been given to them but put a lower price on one they did not yet own.

Gaussian adaptation

Gaussian adaptation is an evolutionary algorithm designed for the maximization of manufacturing yield due to statistical deviation of component values of signal processing systems. In short, Gaussian adaptation is a stochastic adaptive process where a number of samples of an n-dimensional vector $x[x^T = (x_1, x_2, .. x_n)]$ are taken from a multivariate Gaussian distribution, N (m, M), having mean m and moment matrix M. The samples are tested for fail or pass. The first- and second-order moments of the Gaussian restricted to the pass samples are m* and M*.

Loss aversion

In prospect theory, Loss aversion refers to people`s tendency to strongly prefer avoiding losses to acquiring gains. Some studies suggest that losses are twice as powerful, psychologically, as gains. Loss aversion was first convincingly demonstrated by Amos Tversky and Daniel Kahneman.

Capital structure

In finance, Capital structure refers to the way a corporation finances its assets through some combination of equity, debt, a firm that sells $20 billion in equity and $80 billion in debt is said to be 20% equity-financed and 80% debt-financed.

United States

The United States of America (commonly referred to as the United States, the U.S., the United StatesA, or America) is a federal constitutional republic comprising fifty states and a federal district. The country is situated mostly in central North America, where its forty-eight contiguous states and Washington, D.C., the capital district, lie between the Pacific and Atlantic Oceans, bordered by Canada to the north and Mexico to the south. The state of Alaska is in the northwest of the continent, with Canada to its east and Russia to the west across the Bering Strait.

Chapter 7. LINKING NEW TECHNOLOGY AND NOVEL CUSTOMER NEEDS

Market	A Market is any one of a variety of different systems, institutions, procedures, social relations and infrastructures whereby persons trade, and goods and services are exchanged, forming part of the economy. It is an arrangement that allows buyers and sellers to exchange things. Markets vary in size, range, geographic scale, location, types and variety of human communities, as well as the types of goods and services traded.
Positioning	In marketing, positioning has come to mean the process by which marketers try to create an image or identity in the minds of their target market for its product, brand, or organization. It is the `relative competitive comparison` their product occupies in a given market as perceived by the target market. Re-positioning involves changing the identity of a product, relative to the identity of competing products, in the collective minds of the target market.
Genetic programming	In artificial intelligence, Genetic programming is an evolutionary algorithm-based methodology inspired by biological evolution to find computer programs that perform a user-defined task. It is a specialization of genetic algorithms (GA) where each individual is a computer program. It is a machine learning technique used to optimize a population of computer programs according to a fitness landscape determined by a program`s ability to perform a given computational task.
Generalized processor sharing	Generalized processor sharing was developed as a service discipline to share the capacity of congested communications links in an efficient, flexible and fair manner. It is not possible to implement Generalized processor sharing exactly since it assumes fluid traffic , but Generalized processor sharing is useful as a benchmark against which realizable service disciplines can be measured. There are several service disciplines which track the performance of Generalized processor sharing quite closely such as weighted fair queuing (WFQ) also known as packet-by-packet Generalized processor sharing.
Discounted cash flow	In finance, Discounted cash flow analysis is a method of valuing a project, company, or asset using the concepts of the time value of money. All future cash flows are estimated and discounted to give their present values (PVs) - the sum of all future cash flows, both incoming and outgoing, is the net present value (NPV), which is taken as the value or price of the cash flows in question. Using Discounted cash flow analysis to compute the NPV takes as input cash flows and a discount rate and gives as output a price; the opposite process - taking cash flows and a price and inferring a discount rate, is called the yield.

Financial analysis	Financial analysis refers to an assessment of the viability, stability and profitability of a business, sub-business or project. It is performed by professionals who prepare reports using ratios that make use of information taken from financial statements and other reports. These reports are usually presented to top management as one of their bases in making business decisions. Based on these reports, management may: · Continue or discontinue its main operation or part of its business; · Make or purchase certain materials in the manufacture of its product; · Acquire or rent/lease certain machineries and equipment in the production of its goods; · Issue stocks or negotiate for a bank loan to increase its working capital; · Make decisions regarding investing or lending capital; · Other decisions that allow management to make an informed selection on various alternatives in the conduct of its business goals.
Fixed costs	In economics, Fixed costs are business expenses that are not dependent on the level of goods or services produced by the business They tend to be time-related, such as salaries or rents being paid per month. This is in contrast to variable costs, which are volume-related. In management accounting, Fixed costs are defined as expenses that do not change as a function of the activity of a business, within the relevant period.
Net present value	In finance, the Net present value of a time series of cash flows, both incoming and outgoing, is defined as the sum of the present values (PVs) of the individual cash flows. In the case when all future cash flows are incoming and the only outflow of cash is the purchase price, the Net present value is simply the PV of future cash flows minus the purchase price . Net present value is a central tool in discounted cash flow (DCF) analysis, and is a standard method for using the time value of money to appraise long-term projects.

Shareholder value	Shareholder value is a business buzz term, which implies that the ultimate measure of a company`s success is to enrich shareholders. It became popular during the 1980s, and is particularly associated with former CEO of General Electric, Jack Welch. In March 2009, Welch openly turned his back on the concept, calling Shareholder value `the dumbest idea in the world`. The term used in several ways: · To refer to the market capitalization of a company (rarely used) · To refer to the concept that the primary goal for a company is to increase the wealth of its shareholders (owners) by paying dividends and/or causing the stock price to increase · To refer to the more specific concept that planned actions by management and the returns to shareholders should outperform certain bench-marks such as the cost of capital concept.
Sunk costs	In economics and business decision-making, Sunk costs are retrospective (past) costs that have already been incurred and cannot be recovered. Sunk costs are sometimes contrasted with prospective costs, which are future costs that may be incurred or changed if an action is taken. Both retrospective and prospective costs may be either fixed (that is, they are not dependent on the volume of economic activity, however measured) or variable (dependent on volume).
Planning	Planning in organizations and public policy is both the organizational process of creating and maintaining a plan; and the psychological process of thinking about the activities required to create a desired goal on some scale. As such, it is a fundamental property of intelligent behavior. This thought process is essential to the creation and refinement of a plan, or integration of it with other plans, that is, it combines forecasting of developments with the preparation of scenarios of how to react to them.
Hedge fund	A Hedge fund is an investment fund open to a limited range of investors that is permitted by regulators to undertake a wider range of investment and trading activities than other investment funds, and that, in general, pays a performance fee to its investment manager. Every Hedge fund has its own investment strategy that determines the type of investments and the methods of investment it undertakes. Hedge funds, as a class, invest in a broad range of investments including shares, debt and commodities.

Chapter 7. LINKING NEW TECHNOLOGY AND NOVEL CUSTOMER NEEDS

Continuous

In probability theory, a probability distribution is called continuous if its cumulative distribution function is continuous . This is equivalent to saying that for random variables X with the distribution in question, Pr[X = a] = 0 for all real numbers a, i.e.: the probability that X attains the value a is zero, for any number a. If the distribution of X is continuous then X is called a continuous random variable.

Economic profit

In neoclassical economics, economic profit is the difference between a firm`s total revenue and its opportunity costs. In classical economics profit is the return to the employer of capital stock in any productive pursuit involving labor. These two definitions are actually the same.

Profit maximization

In economics, Profit maximization is the process by which a firm determines the price and output level that returns the greatest profit. There are several approaches to this problem. The total revenue-total cost method relies on the fact that profit equals revenue minus cost, and the marginal revenue-marginal cost method is based on the fact that total profit in a perfectly competitive market reaches its maximum point where marginal revenue equals marginal cost.

Gross margin

Gross margin is the difference between the sales and the production costs excluding overhead, payroll, taxation, and interest payments. Gross margin can be defined as the amount of contribution to the business enterprise, after paying for direct-fixed and direct-variable unit costs, required to cover overheads (fixed commitments) and provide a buffer for unknown items. It expresses the relationship between gross profit and sales revenue. It is a measure of how well each dollar of a company`s revenue is utilized to cover the costs of goods sold.

Project charter

In project management, a Project charter is a statement of the scope, objectives and participants in a project. It provides a preliminary delineation of roles and responsibilities, outlines the project objectives, identifies the main stakeholders, and defines the authority of the project manager. It serves as a reference of authority for the future of the project.

Checklist

A Checklist is a type of informational job aid used to reduce failure by compensating for potential limits of human memory and attention. It helps to ensure consistency and completeness in carrying out a task. A basic example is the `to do list.` A more advanced Checklist would be a schedule, which lays out tasks to be done according to time of day or other factors.

Niche market

A Niche market is the subset of the market on which a specific product is focusing; therefore the market niche defines the specific product features aimed at satisfying specific market needs, as well as the price range, production quality and the demographics that is intended to impact.

	Every single product that is on sale can be defined by its Niche market. As of special note, the products aimed at a wide demographic audience, with the resulting low price , are said to belong to the mainstream niche--in practice referred to only as mainstream or of high demand.
Single version of the truth	In computerized business management, Single version of the truth is a technical concept describing the data warehousing ideal of having either a single centralised database, or at least a distributed synchronised database, which stores all of an organisation`s data in a consistent and non-redundant form. In some systems and in the context of message processing systems (often realtime systems), this term also refers to the goal of establishing a single agreed sequence of messages within a database formed by a particular but arbitrary sequencing of records. The key concept is that data combined in a certain sequence is a `truth` which may be analyzed and processed giving particular results, and that although the sequence is arbitrary (and thus another correct but equally arbitrary sequencing would ultimately provide different results in any analysis), it is desirable to agree that the sequence enshrined in the `Single version of the truth` is the version that will be considered `the truth`, and that any conclusions drawn from analysis of the database are valid and unarguable, and (in a technical context) the database may be duplicated to a backup environment to ensure a persistent record is kept of the `Single version of the truth`.
Goal	A Goal or objective is a projected state of affairs that a person or a system plans or intends to achieve--a personal or organizational desired end-point in some sort of assumed development. Many people endeavor to reach Goals within a finite time by setting deadlines. A desire or an intention becomes a Goal if and only if one activates an action for achieving it .
Market development	A Market development strategy targets non-buying customers in currently targeted segments. It also targets new customers in new segments. A marketing manager has to think about the following questions before implementing a Market development strategy: Is it profitable? Will it require the introduction of new or modified products? Is the customer and channel well enough researched and understood? The marketing manager uses these four groups to give more focus to the market segment decision: existing customers, competitor customers, non-buying in current segments, new segments.

Market share	Market share, in strategic management and marketing is, according to Carlton O`Neal, the percentage or proportion of the total available market or market segment that is being serviced by a company. It can be expressed as a company`s sales revenue (from that market) divided by the total sales revenue available in that market. It can also be expressed as a company`s unit sales volume (in a market) divided by the total volume of units sold in that market.
Aggregate Project Plan	An Aggregate Project Plan is the process of creating development goals and objectives and using these goals and objectives to improve productivity as well as development capabilities. The purpose of this process is generally to ensure that each project will accomplish its development goals and objectives. Projects can be differentiated into five types of projects: breakthrough, platform, derivative, R'D, or partnered projects (such as projects performed with partners or allianced firms).
Economic value	The Economic value of a good or service has puzzled economists since the beginning of the discipline. First, economists tried to estimate the value of a good to an individual alone, and extend that definition to goods which can be exchanged. From this analysis came the concepts value in use and value in exchange.Wealth maximization predicts that a person will choose to obtain the good or service in the place where it is cheapest, where the amount given up is the least.Value is linked to price through the mechanism of exchange. When an economist observes an exchange, two important value functions are revealed: those of the buyer and seller. Just as the buyer reveals what he is willing to pay for a certain amount of a good, so too does the seller reveal what it costs him to give up the good.
Value chain	The Value chain is a concept from business management that was first described and popularized by Michael Porter in his 1985 best-seller, Competitive Advantage: Creating and Sustaining Superior Performance. A Value chain is a chain of activities for a firm operating in a specific industry. The business unit is the appropriate level for construction of a Value chain, not the divisional level or corporate level.
Competitive advantage	Competitive advantage is a position of a company in a competitive landscape that allows the company earning return on investments higher than the cost of investments. Competitive advantage should be relevant, unique, and sustainable. Competitive advantage is a theory that seeks to address some of the criticisms of comparative advantage.

First-mover advantage	First-mover advantage is the advantage gained by the initial occupant of a market segment. This advantage may stem from the fact that the first entrant can gain control of resources that followers may not be able to match. Sometimes the first mover is not able to capitalise on its advantage, leaving the opportunity for another firm to gain second-mover advantage.
Camera	A Camera is a device that records images, either as a still photograph or as moving images known as videos or movies. The term comes from the Camera obscura , an early mechanism of projecting images where an entire room functioned as a real-time imaging system; the modern Camera evolved from the Camera obscura. Cameras may work with the light of the visible spectrum or with other portions of the electromagnetic spectrum.
Customer intimacy	Customer intimacy is a concept from marketing, which describes the ability of a supplier to become accepted and known as the regular partner with its customer. Customer intimacy creates a virtuous circle: the better the supplier knows the customer company with its objectives and difficulties, the better able he is to provide an optimal solution. The more adapted the supplier`s product or service is, the happier the customer will be, and the stronger the `intimacy` between the two parties.
Operational definition	An Operational definition is a demonstration of a process - such as a variable, term, or object - in terms of the specific process or set of validation tests used to determine its presence and quantity. The term was coined by Percy Williams Bridgman . Properties described in this manner must be sufficiently accessible, so that persons other than the definer may independently measure or test for them at will.
Operational excellence	Operational excellence is a philosophy of leadership, teamwork and problem solving resulting in continuous improvement throughout the organization by focusing on the needs of the customer, empowering employees, and optimizing existing activities in the process. Operational excellence stresses the need to continually improve by promoting a stronger teamwork atmosphere. Safety and quality improvements for employees and customers lead towards becoming a better enterprise.

Leadership	In response to the criticism of the trait approach, theorists began to research Leadership as a set of behaviors, evaluating the behavior of `successful` leaders, determining a behavior taxonomy and identifying broad Leadership styles. David McClelland, for example, saw Leadership skills, not so much as a set of traits, but as a pattern of motives. He claimed that successful leaders will tend to have a high need for power, a low need for affiliation, and a high level of what he called activity inhibition (one might call it self-control).
Advanced Micro Devices	Advanced Micro Devices, Inc. is an American multinational semiconductor company based in Sunnyvale, California, that develops computer processors and related technologies for commercial and consumer markets. Its main products include microprocessors, motherboard chipsets, embedded processors and graphics processors for servers, workstations and personal computers, and processor technologies for handheld devices, digital television, automobiles, game consoles, and other embedded systems applications.
King	A King is a head of state, who may or may not, depending on the style of government of a nation, exercise monarchal powers over a nation, usually called a Kingdom or a realm. A King is the second highest sovereign title, only looKing up to an emperor. The female equivalent of King is queen; although the term `queen` may refer to one ruling as a monarch in her own right, a queen regnant, or to the wife of a King, a queen consort.
Market dominance	Market dominance is a measure of the strength of a brand, product, service, relative to competitive offerings. There is often a geographic element to the competitive landscape. In defining Market dominance, you must see to what extent a product, brand, or firm controls a product category in a given geographic area.
Customer service	Customer service is the provision of service to customers before, during and after a purchase. According to Jamier L. Scott. (2002), `Customer service is a series of activities designed to enhance the level of customer satisfaction - that is, the feeling that a product or service has met the customer expectation.` Its importance varies by product, industry and customer; defective or broken merchandise can be exchanged, often only with a receipt and within a specified time frame.

Mass customization	Mass customization, in marketing, manufacturing, call centres and management, is the use of flexible computer-aided manufacturing systems to produce custom output. Those systems combine the low unit costs of mass production processes with the flexibility of individual customization. `Mass customization` is the new frontier in business competition for both manufacturing and service industries.

Chapter 8. INTERNAL CORPORATE VENTURING

Case study	A Case study is one of several ways of doing research whether it is social science related or even socially related. It is an intensive study of a single group, incident, or community. Other ways include experiments, surveys, or analysis of archival information.
Concepts	Kant declared that human minds possess pure or a priori concepts. Instead of being abstracted from individual perceptions, like empirical concepts, they originate in the mind itself. He called these concepts categories, in the sense of the word that means predicate, attribute, characteristic, or quality.
Group	In business, a group, business group, corporate group) alliance is most commonly a legal entity that is a type of conglomerate or holding company consisting of a parent company and subsidiaries. Typical examples are Adidas group or Icelandair group. In United Arab Emirates, Business group can also be knows as Trade association.
Camera	A Camera is a device that records images, either as a still photograph or as moving images known as videos or movies. The term comes from the Camera obscura , an early mechanism of projecting images where an entire room functioned as a real-time imaging system; the modern Camera evolved from the Camera obscura. Cameras may work with the light of the visible spectrum or with other portions of the electromagnetic spectrum.
Centralization	Centralisation is the process by which the activities of an organisation, particularly those regarding Planing decision-making, become concentrated within a particular location and/or group. In political science, this refers to the concentration of a government`s power - both geographically and politically, into a centralised government. In neuroscience, centralization refers to the evolutionary trend of the nervous system to be partitioned into a central nervous system and peripheral nervous system.

Enterprise resource planning	Enterprise resource planning is an Integrated computer-based system used to manage internal and external resources, including tangible assets, financial resources, materials, and human resources. It is a software architecture whose purpose is to facilitate the flow of information between all business functions inside the boundaries of the organization and manage the connections to outside stakeholders. Built on a centralized database and normally utilizing a common computing platform, Enterprise resource planning systems consolidate all business operations into a uniform and enterprise-wide system environment.
Planning	Planning in organizations and public policy is both the organizational process of creating and maintaining a plan; and the psychological process of thinking about the activities required to create a desired goal on some scale. As such, it is a fundamental property of intelligent behavior. This thought process is essential to the creation and refinement of a plan, or integration of it with other plans, that is, it combines forecasting of developments with the preparation of scenarios of how to react to them.
Resources	A resource is any physical or virtual entity of limited availability, or anything used to help one earn a living. In most cases, commercial or even ethic factors require resource allocation through resource management. As resources are very useful, we attach some information value to them.
Business process	A Business process or business method is a collection of related, structured activities or tasks that produce a specific service or product for a particular customer or customers. It often can be visualized with a flowchart as a sequence of activities. Overview There are three types of Business processes: · Management processes, the processes that govern the operation of a system. Typical management processes include `Corporate Governance` and `Strategic Management`. · Operational processes, processes that constitute the core business and create the primary value stream. Typical operational processes are Purchasing, Manufacturing, Marketing and Sales. · Supporting processes, which support the core processes. Examples include Accounting, Recruitment, Technical support.
Data warehouse	Data warehouse is a repository of an organization`s electronically stored data. Data warehouses are designed to facilitate reporting and analysis.

A Data warehouse houses a standardized, consistent, clean and integrated form of data sourced from various operational systems in use in the organization, structured in a way to specifically address the reporting and analytic requirements.

Short-run

In economics, the concept of the Short-run refers to the decision-making time frame of a firm in which at least one factor of production is fixed. Costs which are fixed in the Short-run have no impact on a firm decisions. For example a firm can raise output by increasing the amount of labor through overtime.

A generic firm can make three changes in the Short-run:

· Increase production

· Decrease production

· Shut down

In the Short-run, a profit maximizing firm will:

· Increase production if marginal cost is less than price;

· Decrease production if marginal cost is greater than price;

· Continue producing if average variable cost is less than price, even if average total cost is greater than price;

· Shut down if average variable cost is greater than price.

Venture capital

Venture capital is provided as seed funding to early-stage, high-potential, growth companies and more often after the seed funding round as growth funding round (also referred as series A round) in the interest of generating a return through an eventual realization event such as an IPO or trade sale of the company. To put it simply, an investment firm will give money to a growing company. The growing company will then use this money to advertise, do research, build infrastructure, develop products etc.

Enabling	Enabling is a term with a double meaning. As a positive term, it references patterns of interaction which allow individuals to develop and grow. These may be on any scale, for example within the family, or in wider society as `Enabling acts` designed to empower some group, or create a new authority for a (usually governmental) body.
Farm	A farm is an area of land, including various structures, devoted primarily to the practice of producing and managing food (produce, grains), fibers and, increasingly, fuel. It is the basic production facility in food production. farms may be owned and operated by a single individual, family, community, corporation or a company.
Mass customization	Mass customization, in marketing, manufacturing, call centres and management, is the use of flexible computer-aided manufacturing systems to produce custom output. Those systems combine the low unit costs of mass production processes with the flexibility of individual customization. `Mass customization` is the new frontier in business competition for both manufacturing and service industries.
Sliced inverse regression	Sliced inverse regression is a tool for dimension reduction in the field of multivariate statistics. In statistics, regression analysis is a popular way of studying the relationship between a response variable y and its explanatory variable $\underline{x}$, which is a p-dimensional vector. There are several approaches which come under the term of regression. We know parametric methods, such as multiple linear regression, but also non-parametric techniques, such as local smoothing. If we have high-dimensional data, the number of observations needed to use local smoothing methods escalates exponentially. Therefore we need a tool for dimension reduction, which reveals us the most important directions of the data, on which it can be projected without losing, in the best case, any information. Sliced inverse regression uses the inverse regression curve, $E(\underline{x}\,\|\,y)$, which falls into the effective dimension reducing space under certain conditions, to perform a weighted principal component analysis, with which one identifies the effective dimension reducing directions.

Xerox	Xerox Corporation is a global document management company which manufactures and sells a range of color and black-and-white printers, multifunction systems, photo copiers, digital production printing presses, and related consulting services and supplies. Xerox is headquartered in Norwalk, Connecticut , though its largest population of employees is based in and around Rochester, New York, the area in which the company was founded. The Xerox 914 was the first one-piece plain paper photocopier, and sold in the thousands. Xerox was founded in 1906 in Rochester, New York as `The Haloid Company`, which originally manufactured photographic paper and equipment.
Demand	In economics, Demand is the desire to own anything and the ability to pay for it and willigness to pay . The term Demand signifies the ability or the willingness to buy a particular commodity at a given point of time. Demand is also defined elsewhere as a measure of preferences that is weighted by income.
Team	A team comprises a group of people or animals linked in a common purpose. teams are especially appropriate for conducting tasks that are high in complexity and have many interdependent subtasks. A group in itself does not necessarily constitute a team.
Innovation	Innovation is a change in the thought process for doing something or `new stuff that is made useful`. It may refer to an incremental emergent or radical and revolutionary changes in thinking, products, processes, or organizations. Following Schumpeter (1934), contributors to the scholarly literature on Innovation typically distinguish between invention, an idea made manifest, and Innovation, ideas applied successfully in practice.
Consultative selling	Consultative selling is an approach to selling based on a dialogue between the salesperson and the customer. First, the customer is encouraged to express his/her needs. The salesperson then selects the product or service that best meets these needs and adapts the sales message to the customer`s needs and language.
Mission statement	A Mission statement is a formal, short, written statement of the purpose of a company or organization. The Mission statement should guide the actions of the organization, spell out its overall goal, provide a sense of direction, and guide decision-making. It provides `the framework or context within which the company`s strategies are formulated.` Historically it is associated with Christian religious groups; indeed, for many years, a missionary was assumed to be a person on a specifically religious mission.

Economic value

The Economic value of a good or service has puzzled economists since the beginning of the discipline. First, economists tried to estimate the value of a good to an individual alone, and extend that definition to goods which can be exchanged. From this analysis came the concepts value in use and value in exchange.Wealth maximization predicts that a person will choose to obtain the good or service in the place where it is cheapest, where the amount given up is the least.Value is linked to price through the mechanism of exchange. When an economist observes an exchange, two important value functions are revealed: those of the buyer and seller. Just as the buyer reveals what he is willing to pay for a certain amount of a good, so too does the seller reveal what it costs him to give up the good.

Hostile work environment

A Hostile work environment exists when an employee experiences workplace harassment and fears going to work because of the offensive, intimidating, religion, sex, national origin, age, disability, veteran status, or, in some jurisdictions, sexual orientation, political affiliation, citizenship status, marital status, or personal appearance. Hostile work environment is also one of the two legal categories of sexual harassment.
A Hostile work environment may also be defined as when a boss or manager begins to engage in a manner designed to make you quit in retaliation for your actions.

Asset

In financial accounting, Assets are economic resources. Anything tangible or intangible that is capable of being owned or controlled to produce value and that is held to have positive economic value is considered an Asset. Simplistically stated, Assets represent ownership of value that can be converted into cash (although cash itself is also considered an Asset).

Complementary assets

Complementary assets are assets, infrastructure or capabilities needed to support the successful commercialization and marketing of a technological innovation, other than those assets fundamentally associated with that innovation. The term was first coined by David Teece. Key empirical studies on Complementary assets were conducted by Frank T. Rothaermel. Complementary assets are broken down into three general types:

· Generic assets: `general purpose` assets which do not need to be tailored to a particular innovation;

· Specialized assets: unilateral dependence between the innovation and the complementary asset;

	· Cospecialized assets: bilateral dependence between the innovation and the complementary asset.
Gold Star	The Gold Star medal is a special insignia that identifies recipients of the title `Hero` in the Soviet Union and several post-Soviet states. The Gold Star was established by the decree of the Presidium of the Supreme Soviet on August 1, 1939. Previously, Heroes of the Soviet Union were awarded the Order of Lenin and a special diploma (gramota, Ð³Ñ€Ð°Ð¼Ð¾Ñ‚Ð°) describing the heroic feat. The medal was introduced to distinguish these heroes from other Order of Lenin recipients.
Market	A Market is any one of a variety of different systems, institutions, procedures, social relations and infrastructures whereby persons trade, and goods and services are exchanged, forming part of the economy. It is an arrangement that allows buyers and sellers to exchange things. Markets vary in size, range, geographic scale, location, types and variety of human communities, as well as the types of goods and services traded.
Market requirements document	A market requirements document in project management and systems engineering, is a document that express the customer`s wants and needs for the product or service.
Thinsulate	Thinsulate is a trademark of the 3M Corporation, for a type of synthetic fiber thermal insulation used in clothing. The word is a portmanteau of thin and insulate. The material was first sold in 1979.
Nominative determinism	Nominative determinism refers to the theory that a person`s name is given an influential role in reflecting key attributes of his job, profession, but real examples are more highly prized, the more obscure the better.
Six Sigma	Six Sigma is a business management strategy originally developed by Motorola, USA in 1981. As of 2010, it enjoys widespread application in many sectors of industry, although its application is not without controversy. Six Sigma seeks to improve the quality of process outputs by identifying and removing the causes of defects (errors) and minimizing variability in manufacturing and business processes. It uses a set of quality management methods, including statistical methods, and creates a special infrastructure of people within the organization (`Black Belts`, `Green Belts`, etc).

Design for Six Sigma	Design for Six Sigma is a separate and emerging business-process management methodology related to traditional Six Sigma. While the tools and order used in Six Sigma require a process to be in place and functioning, Design for Six Sigma has the objective of determining the needs of customers and the business, and driving those needs into the product solution so created. Design for Six Sigma is relevant to the complex system/product synthesis phase, especially in the context of unprecedented system development.
Process model	The term process model is used in various contexts. For example, in business process modeling the enterprise process model is often referred to as the business process model. process models are core concepts in the discipline of Process Engineering.
Models	Experience curve re-directs here. For its use in video games see Experience point. Models of the learning curve effect and the closely related experience curve effect express the relationship between equations for experience and efficiency or between efficiency gains and investment in the effort.
File sharing	File sharing is the practice of distributing or providing access to digitally stored information, such as computer programs, multi-media (audio, video), documents, transmission, and distribution models. Common methods are manual sharing using removable media, centralized computer file server installations on computer networks, World Wide Web-based hyperlinked documents, and the use of distributed peer-to-peer (P2P) networking.
Volkswagen	The Volkswagen Automobile Company is an automobile manufacturer based in Wolfsburg, Germany, and is the original brand within the Volkswagen Group, as well as the largest brand by sales volume. Volkswagen means `people`s car` in German, in which it is pronounced . Its current tagline or slogan is Das Auto .
Market dominance	Market dominance is a measure of the strength of a brand, product, service, relative to competitive offerings. There is often a geographic element to the competitive landscape. In defining Market dominance, you must see to what extent a product, brand, or firm controls a product category in a given geographic area.
Dominant design	Dominant Design is a Technology Management concept identifying key technological designs that become a de-facto standard in their market place. When a new technology emerges (e.g. computer GUI operating systems) - often firms will introduce a number of alternative designs (e.g. Microsoft - Windows, Apple Inc. - Mac OS and IBM - OS2) .

Chapter 8. INTERNAL CORPORATE VENTURING

Competitive advantage	Competitive advantage is a position of a company in a competitive landscape that allows the company earning return on investments higher than the cost of investments. Competitive advantage should be relevant, unique, and sustainable. Competitive advantage is a theory that seeks to address some of the criticisms of comparative advantage.
Customer service	Customer service is the provision of service to customers before, during and after a purchase. According to Jamier L. Scott. (2002), `Customer service is a series of activities designed to enhance the level of customer satisfaction - that is, the feeling that a product or service has met the customer expectation.` Its importance varies by product, industry and customer; defective or broken merchandise can be exchanged, often only with a receipt and within a specified time frame.
Leadership	In response to the criticism of the trait approach, theorists began to research Leadership as a set of behaviors, evaluating the behavior of `successful` leaders, determining a behavior taxonomy and identifying broad Leadership styles. David McClelland, for example, saw Leadership skills, not so much as a set of traits, but as a pattern of motives. He claimed that successful leaders will tend to have a high need for power, a low need for affiliation, and a high level of what he called activity inhibition (one might call it self-control).
Aggregate planning	Aggregate planning is an operational activity that does an aggregate plan for the production process, in advance of 2 to 18 months, to give an idea to management as to what quantity of materials and other resources are to be procured and when, so that the total cost of operations of the organization is kept to the minimum over that period. The quantity of outsourcing, subcontracting of items, overtime of labour, numbers to be hired and fired in each period and the amount of inventory to be held in stock and to be backlogged for each period are decided. All of these activities are done within the framework of the company ethics, policies, and long term commitment to the society, community and the country of operation.

Management Development	Management Development is best described as the process from which managers learn and improve their skills not only to benefit themselves but also their employing organizations. In organisational development (OD), the effectiveness of management is recognised as one of the determinants of organisational success. Therefore, investment in Management Development can have a direct economic benefit to the organization.
Partnership	Partnerships may be formed in the legal forms of General partnership (Offene Handelsgesellschaft, OHG) or Limited partnership (Kommanditgesellschaft, KG). A partnership can be formed by only one person. In the OHG, all partners are fully liable for the partnership`s debts, whereas in the KG there are general partners with unlimited liability and limited partners whose liability is restricted to their fixed contributions to the partnership.
Inventory	Inventory is a list for goods and materials, or those goods and materials themselves, held available in stock by a business. It is also used for a list of the contents of a household and for a list for testamentary purposes of the possessions of someone who has died. In accounting Inventory is considered an asset.
Tiger team	A Tiger team is a specialized group that tests an organization`s ability to protect its assets by attempting to circumvent, defeat, or otherwise thwart that organization`s internal and external security. The term is also used in other settings, including information technology, aerospace design, and emergency management. The term originated within the military to describe a team whose purpose is to penetrate security of `friendly` installations to test security measures.
Quality function deployment	Quality function deployment is a `method to transform user demands into design quality, to deploy the functions forming quality, and to deploy methods for achieving the design quality into subsystems and component parts, and ultimately to specific elements of the manufacturing process.` , as described by Dr. Yoji Akao, who originally developed Quality function deployment in Japan in 1966, when the author combined his work in quality assurance and quality control points with function deployment used in Value Engineering. Quality function deployment is designed to help planners focus on characteristics of a new or existing product or service from the viewpoints of market segments, company, or technology-development needs. The technique yields graphs and matrices.

Audit	The general definition of an Audit is an evaluation of a person, organization, system, process, enterprise, project or product. The term most commonly refers to Audits in accounting, but similar concepts also exist in project management, quality management, and for energy conservation. Audits are performed to ascertain the validity and reliability of information; also to provide an assessment of a system`s internal control. The goal of an Audit is to express an opinion on the person / organization / system (etc) in question, under evaluation based on work done on a test basis. Due to practical constraints, an Audit seeks to provide only reasonable assurance that the statements are free from material error. Hence, statistical sampling is often adopted in Audits. In the case of financial Audits, a set of financial statements are said to be true and fair when they are free of material misstatements - a concept influenced by both quantitative and qualitative factors.

Communications management	Communications management is the systematic planning, implementing, monitoring, and revision of all the channels of communication within an organization, and between organizations; it also includes the organization and dissemination of new communication directives connected with an organization, network, designing internal and external communications directives, and managing the flow of information, including online communication. New technology forces constant innovation on the part of communications managers.
Tuple	In mathematics and computer science a Tuple represents the notion of an ordered list of elements. In set theory, an (ordered) *n*-Tuple is a sequence (or ordered list) of *n* elements, where *n* is a positive integer. There is also one 0-Tuple, an empty sequence.
Market dominance	Market dominance is a measure of the strength of a brand, product, service, relative to competitive offerings. There is often a geographic element to the competitive landscape. In defining Market dominance, you must see to what extent a product, brand, or firm controls a product category in a given geographic area.
Change request	A change request is a document containing a call for an adjustment of a system; it is of great importance in the change management process. A change request is not raised for a wording change in a letter. A change request is declarative, i.e. it states what needs to be accomplished, but leaves out how the change should be carried out.
Innovation	Innovation is a change in the thought process for doing something or `new stuff that is made useful`. It may refer to an incremental emergent or radical and revolutionary changes in thinking, products, processes, or organizations. Following Schumpeter (1934), contributors to the scholarly literature on Innovation typically distinguish between invention, an idea made manifest, and Innovation, ideas applied successfully in practice.
Inventory	Inventory is a list for goods and materials, or those goods and materials themselves, held available in stock by a business. It is also used for a list of the contents of a household and for a list for testamentary purposes of the possessions of someone who has died. In accounting Inventory is considered an asset.
Trade-off	A Trade-off is a situation that involves losing one quality or aspect of something in return for gaining another quality or aspect. It implies a decision to be made with full comprehension of both the upside and downside of a particular choice.

	In economics the term is expressed as opportunity cost, referring to the most preferred alternative given up.
Enterprise resource planning	Enterprise resource planning is an Integrated computer-based system used to manage internal and external resources, including tangible assets, financial resources, materials, and human resources. It is a software architecture whose purpose is to facilitate the flow of information between all business functions inside the boundaries of the organization and manage the connections to outside stakeholders. Built on a centralized database and normally utilizing a common computing platform, Enterprise resource planning systems consolidate all business operations into a uniform and enterprise-wide system environment.
Case study	A Case study is one of several ways of doing research whether it is social science related or even socially related. It is an intensive study of a single group, incident, or community. Other ways include experiments, surveys, or analysis of archival information.
File sharing	File sharing is the practice of distributing or providing access to digitally stored information, such as computer programs, multi-media (audio, video), documents, transmission, and distribution models. Common methods are manual sharing using removable media, centralized computer file server installations on computer networks, World Wide Web-based hyperlinked documents, and the use of distributed peer-to-peer (P2P) networking.
New product development	In business and engineering, New product development is the term used to describe the complete process of bringing a new product or service to market. There are two parallel paths involved in the New product development process: one involves the idea generation, product design and detail engineering; the other involves market research and marketing analysis. Companies typically see New product development as the first stage in generating and commercializing new products within the overall strategic process of product life cycle management used to maintain or grow their market share.
Group	In business, a group, business group, corporate group) alliance is most commonly a legal entity that is a type of conglomerate or holding company consisting of a parent company and subsidiaries. Typical examples are Adidas group or Icelandair group. In United Arab Emirates, Business group can also be knows as Trade association.

Synthetic environment	Synthetic environment refers to simulations on the internet that represent activities at a high level of realism, from simulations of theaters of war to factories and manufacturing processes. These environments may be created within a single computer or a vast distributed network connected by local and wide area networks and augmented by super-realistic special effects and accurate behavioral models. Synthetic environment allows visualization of and immersion into the environment being simulated. The Synthetic environment could be divided into the terms below to eliminate ambiguity and confusion: · Synthetic natural environment - Representation of climate, weather, terrain, oceans, space, etc. · Synthetic human-made environment - Representation of human-made structures like buildings, bridges, and roads · Synthetic psychological environment - Representation of psychological influences on individuals and/or groups based on demography and other cultural factors.
Venture capital	Venture capital is provided as seed funding to early-stage, high-potential, growth companies and more often after the seed funding round as growth funding round (also referred as series A round) in the interest of generating a return through an eventual realization event such as an IPO or trade sale of the company. To put it simply, an investment firm will give money to a growing company. The growing company will then use this money to advertise, do research, build infrastructure, develop products etc.
Estrogen	Estrogens (U.S., otherwise oEstrogens or Å"strogens) are a group of steroid compounds and functioning as the primary female sex hormone, their name comes from estrus/oistros (period of fertility for female mammals) + gen/gonos = to generate. Estrogens are used as part of some oral contraceptives, in Estrogen replacement therapy for postmenopausal women, and in hormone replacement therapy for transwomen. Like all steroid hormones, Estrogens readily diffuse across the cell membrane.

Chapter 9. NEW PRODUCT DEVELOPMENT

Organizational chart	An Organizational chart (often called organization chart, org chart, organigram, or organogram (me)) is a diagram that shows the structure of an organization and the relationships and relative ranks of its parts and positions/jobs. The term is also used for similar diagrams, for example ones showing the different elements of a field of knowledge or a group of languages. The French Encyclopédie had one of the first Organizational charts of knowledge in general.
Insulin	Insulin is a hormone that has extensive effects on metabolism and other body functions, such as vascular compliance. Insulin causes cells in the liver, muscle, and fat tissue to take up glucose from the blood, storing it as glycogen in the liver and muscle, and stopping use of fat as an energy source. When Insulin is absent (or low), glucose is not taken up by body cells, and the body begins to use fat as an energy source, for example, by transfer of lipids from adipose tissue to the liver for mobilization as an energy source.
Research and development	The phrase Research and development according to the Organization for Economic Co-operation and Development, refers to `creative work undertaken on a systematic basis in order to increase the stock of knowledge, including knowledge of man, culture and society, and the use of this stock of knowledge to devise new applications`.
	New product design and development is more often than not a crucial factor in the survival of a company. In an industry that is fast changing, firms must continually revise their design and range of products.
Intellectual property	Intellectual property is a term referring to a number of distinct types of creations of the mind for which property rights are recognised--and the corresponding fields of law. Under Intellectual property law, owners are granted certain exclusive rights to a variety of intangible assets, such as musical, literary, and artistic works; discoveries and inventions; and words, phrases, symbols, and designs. Common types of Intellectual property include copyrights, trademarks, patents, industrial design rights and trade secrets in some jurisdictions.
First-mover advantage	First-mover advantage is the advantage gained by the initial occupant of a market segment. This advantage may stem from the fact that the first entrant can gain control of resources that followers may not be able to match. Sometimes the first mover is not able to capitalise on its advantage, leaving the opportunity for another firm to gain second-mover advantage.
Brain drain	Brain drain or human capital flight is a large emigration of individuals with technical skills or knowledge, normally due to conflict, lack of opportunity, political instability, since emigrants usually take with them the fraction of value of their training sponsored by the government. It is a parallel of capital flight which refers to the same movement of financial capital.

Chapter 9. NEW PRODUCT DEVELOPMENT

Functional selectivity	Functional selectivity (or \`agonist trafficking\`, \`biased agonism\`, \`differential engagement\` and \`protean agonism\`) is the ligand-dependent selectivity for certain signal transduction pathways in one and the same receptor. This can be present when a receptor has several possible signal transduction pathways. To which degree each pathway is activated thus depends on which ligand binds to the receptor .
Team	A team comprises a group of people or animals linked in a common purpose. teams are especially appropriate for conducting tasks that are high in complexity and have many interdependent subtasks. A group in itself does not necessarily constitute a team.
Osteoporosis	Osteoporosis is a disease of bone that leads to an increased risk of fracture. In Osteoporosis the bone mineral density (BMD) is reduced, bone microarchitecture is disrupted, and the amount and variety of non-collagenous proteins in bone is altered. Osteoporosis is defined by the World Health Organization (WHO) in women as a bone mineral density 2.5 standard deviations below peak bone mass (20-year-old healthy female average) as measured by DXA; the term \`established Osteoporosis\` includes the presence of a fragility fracture.
Aggregate planning	Aggregate planning is an operational activity that does an aggregate plan for the production process, in advance of 2 to 18 months, to give an idea to management as to what quantity of materials and other resources are to be procured and when, so that the total cost of operations of the organization is kept to the minimum over that period. The quantity of outsourcing, subcontracting of items, overtime of labour, numbers to be hired and fired in each period and the amount of inventory to be held in stock and to be backlogged for each period are decided. All of these activities are done within the framework of the company ethics, policies, and long term commitment to the society, community and the country of operation.
Management Development	Management Development is best described as the process from which managers learn and improve their skills not only to benefit themselves but also their employing organizations. In organisational development (OD), the effectiveness of management is recognised as one of the determinants of organisational success. Therefore, investment in Management Development can have a direct economic benefit to the organization.

Tiger team	A Tiger team is a specialized group that tests an organization`s ability to protect its assets by attempting to circumvent, defeat, or otherwise thwart that organization`s internal and external security. The term is also used in other settings, including information technology, aerospace design, and emergency management. The term originated within the military to describe a team whose purpose is to penetrate security of `friendly` installations to test security measures.
Project charter	In project management, a Project charter is a statement of the scope, objectives and participants in a project. It provides a preliminary delineation of roles and responsibilities, outlines the project objectives, identifies the main stakeholders, and defines the authority of the project manager. It serves as a reference of authority for the future of the project.
Executive sponsor	The role of Executive sponsor is a role in project management, usually the senior member of the project board and often the chair. In smaller organisations the Executive sponsor may also be the project manager but typically the project sponsor will be a senior executive in a corporation (often at or just below board level) who is responsible to the business for the success of the project. Where the role of Executive sponsor exists as a separate role the person in that role rarely becomes involved in the running of the project. Their role centers around: · Advocating the project both internally and externally · Championing the project · Obtaining budgets for the project · Accepting responsibility for problems escalated from the project manager · Signing off documents such as the business case and project initiation document · Supporting the project manager in managing the project

Due to the problem solving needs of the role the Executive sponsor often needs to be able to exert pressure within the organisation to overcome resistance to the project.

Market

A Market is any one of a variety of different systems, institutions, procedures, social relations and infrastructures whereby persons trade, and goods and services are exchanged, forming part of the economy. It is an arrangement that allows buyers and sellers to exchange things. Markets vary in size, range, geographic scale, location, types and variety of human communities, as well as the types of goods and services traded.

Market segmentation

Market segmentation is a concept in economics and marketing. A market segment is a sub-set of a market made up of people or organizations sharing with one or more characteristics that cause them to demand similar product and/or services based on qualities of those products such as price or function. A true market segment meets all of the following criteria: it is distinct from other segments (different segments have different needs), it is homogeneous within the segment (exhibits common needs); it responds similarly to a market stimulus, and it can be reached by a market intervention.

Positioning

In marketing, positioning has come to mean the process by which marketers try to create an image or identity in the minds of their target market for its product, brand, or organization. It is the `relative competitive comparison` their product occupies in a given market as perceived by the target market.

Re-positioning involves changing the identity of a product, relative to the identity of competing products, in the collective minds of the target market.

Business-to-business

Business-to-business describes commerce transactions between businesses, such as between a manufacturer and a wholesaler, or between a wholesaler and a retailer. Contrasting terms are business-to-consumer (B2C) and business-to-government (B2G).

The volume of B2B transactions is much higher than the volume of B2C transactions.

Market research

Market research is any organized effort to gather information about markets or customers. It is a very important component of business strategy. The term is commonly interchanged with marketing research; however, expert practitioners may wish to draw a distinction, in that marketing research is concerned specifically about marketing processes, while Market research is concerned specifically with markets.

Generalized additive model

In statistics, the Generalized additive model is a statistical model developed by Trevor Hastie and Rob Tibshirani for blending properties of generalized linear models with additive models.

The model specifies a distribution (such as a normal distribution, or a binomial distribution) and a link function g relating the expected value of the distribution to the predictors, and attempts to fit functions f_i to satisfy:

$$g(\mathrm{E}(Y)) = \beta_0 + f_1(x_1) + f_2(x_2) + \cdots + f_m(x_m).$$

The functions $f_i(x_i)$ may be fit using parametric or non-parametric means, thus providing the potential for better fits to data than other methods. The method hence is very general - a typical Generalized additive model might use a scatterplot smoothing function such as a locally weighted mean for $f_1(x_1)$, and then use a factor model for $f_2(x_2)$. By allowing nonparametric fits, well designed Generalized additive models allow good fits to the training data with relaxed assumptions on the actual relationship, perhaps at the expense of interpretability of results.

Nominative determinism

Nominative determinism refers to the theory that a person`s name is given an influential role in reflecting key attributes of his job, profession, but real examples are more highly prized, the more obscure the better.

Procter ' Gamble

Procter is a surname, and may also refer to:

· Bryan Waller Procter (pseud. Barry Cornwall), English poet

· Goodwin Procter, American law firm

· Procter ' Gamble, consumer products multinational `

Business plan

A Business plan is a formal statement of a set of business goals, the reasons why they are believed attainable, and the plan for reaching those goals. It may also contain background information about the organization or team attempting to reach those goals.

Marketing

Marketing is a `social and managerial process by which individuals and groups obtain what they need and want through creating and exchanging products and values with others.` It is an integrated process through which companies create value for customers and build strong customer relationships in order to capture value from customers in return.

marketing is used to create the customer, to keep the customer and to satisfy the customer. With the customer as the focus of its activities, it can be concluded that marketing management is one of the major components of business management.

Marketing mix

The term `Marketing mix` was first used in 1953 when Neil Borden, in his American Marketing Association presidential address, took the recipe idea one step further and coined the term `marketing-mix`. A prominent marketer, E. Jerome McCarthy, proposed a 4 P classification in 1960, which has seen wide use. The four Ps concept is explained in most marketing textbooks and classes.

Elements of the Marketing mix are often referred to as `the four Ps`:

· Product - A tangible object or an intangible service that is mass produced or manufactured on a large scale with a specific volume of units. Intangible products are service based like the tourism industry ' the hotel industry or codes-based products like cellphone load and credits. Typical examples of a mass produced tangible object are the motor car and the disposable razor. A less obvious but ubiquitous mass produced service is a computer operating system. Packaging also needs to be taken into consideration.

· Price - The price is the amount a customer pays for the product. It is determined by a number of factors including market share, competition, material costs, product identity and the customer`s perceived value of the product. The business may increase or decrease the price of product if other stores have the same product.

· Place - Place represents the location where a product can be purchased. It is often referred to as the distribution channel. It can include any physical store as well as virtual stores on the Internet. Place is not exatly a physical store where it is available Place is nothing but how the product takes place or creat image in the mind of customers. It`s depend upon the percievedness of customers.

· Promotion represents all of the communications that a marketer may use in the marketplace. Promotion has four distinct elements: advertising, public relations, personal selling and sales promotion. A certain amount of crossover occurs when promotion uses the four principal elements together, which is common in film promotion. Advertising covers any communication that is paid for, from cinema commercials, radio and Internet adverts through print media and billboards. Public relations are where the communication is not directly paid for and includes press releases, sponsorship deals, exhibitions, conferences, seminars or trade fairs and events. Word of mouth is any apparently informal communication about the product by ordinary individuals, satisfied customers or people specifically engaged to create word of mouth momentum. Sales staff often plays an important role in word of mouth and Public Relations .

Camera

A Camera is a device that records images, either as a still photograph or as moving images known as videos or movies. The term comes from the Camera obscura , an early mechanism of projecting images where an entire room functioned as a real-time imaging system; the modern Camera evolved from the Camera obscura.

Cameras may work with the light of the visible spectrum or with other portions of the electromagnetic spectrum.

Chapter 10. BUILDING COMPETENCE/CAPABILITIES THROUGH NEW PRODUCT DEVELOPMENT

Case study	A Case study is one of several ways of doing research whether it is social science related or even socially related. It is an intensive study of a single group, incident, or community. Other ways include experiments, surveys, or analysis of archival information.
Market	A Market is any one of a variety of different systems, institutions, procedures, social relations and infrastructures whereby persons trade, and goods and services are exchanged, forming part of the economy. It is an arrangement that allows buyers and sellers to exchange things. Markets vary in size, range, geographic scale, location, types and variety of human communities, as well as the types of goods and services traded.
Best practice	A Best practice is a technique, method, process, activity, incentive, or reward that is believed to be more effective at delivering a particular outcome than any other technique, method, process, etc. when applied to a particular condition or circumstance. The idea is that with proper processes, checks, and testing, a desired outcome can be delivered with fewer problems and unforeseen complications. Best practices can also be defined as the most efficient (least amount of effort) and effective (best results) way of accomplishing a task, based on repeatable procedures that have proven themselves over time for large numbers of people.
Supply chain	A Supply chain is a system of organizations, people, technology, activities, information and resources involved in moving a product or service from supplier to customer. Supply chain activities transform natural resources, raw materials and components into a finished product that is delivered to the end customer. In sophisticated Supply chain systems, used products may re-enter the Supply chain at any point where residual value is recyclable.
Wheat	Wheat (Triticum spp). is a worldwide cultivated grass from the Fertile Crescent region of the Near East. In 2007 world production of Wheat was 607 million tons, making it the third most-produced cereal after maize (784 million tons) and rice (651 million tons).
Innovation	Innovation is a change in the thought process for doing something or `new stuff that is made useful`. It may refer to an incremental emergent or radical and revolutionary changes in thinking, products, processes, or organizations. Following Schumpeter (1934), contributors to the scholarly literature on Innovation typically distinguish between invention, an idea made manifest, and Innovation, ideas applied successfully in practice.
Project planning	Project planning is part of project management, which relates to the use of schedules such as Gantt charts to plan and subsequently report progress within the project environment.

Initially, the project scope is defined and the appropriate methods for completing the project are determined. Following this step, the durations for the various tasks necessary to complete the work are listed and grouped into a work breakdown structure.

Aggregate planning

Aggregate planning is an operational activity that does an aggregate plan for the production process, in advance of 2 to 18 months, to give an idea to management as to what quantity of materials and other resources are to be procured and when, so that the total cost of operations of the organization is kept to the minimum over that period.

The quantity of outsourcing, subcontracting of items, overtime of labour, numbers to be hired and fired in each period and the amount of inventory to be held in stock and to be backlogged for each period are decided. All of these activities are done within the framework of the company ethics, policies, and long term commitment to the society, community and the country of operation.

Goal

A Goal or objective is a projected state of affairs that a person or a system plans or intends to achieve--a personal or organizational desired end-point in some sort of assumed development. Many people endeavor to reach Goals within a finite time by setting deadlines.
A desire or an intention becomes a Goal if and only if one activates an action for achieving it .

Partnership

Partnerships may be formed in the legal forms of General partnership (Offene Handelsgesellschaft, OHG) or Limited partnership (Kommanditgesellschaft, KG). A partnership can be formed by only one person. In the OHG, all partners are fully liable for the partnership`s debts, whereas in the KG there are general partners with unlimited liability and limited partners whose liability is restricted to their fixed contributions to the partnership.

Procter ' Gamble

Procter is a surname, and may also refer to:

· Bryan Waller Procter (pseud. Barry Cornwall), English poet

· Goodwin Procter, American law firm

· Procter ' Gamble, consumer products multinational `

Chapter 10. BUILDING COMPETENCE/CAPABILITIES THROUGH NEW PRODUCT DEVELOPMENT

Camera	A Camera is a device that records images, either as a still photograph or as moving images known as videos or movies. The term comes from the Camera obscura , an early mechanism of projecting images where an entire room functioned as a real-time imaging system; the modern Camera evolved from the Camera obscura. Cameras may work with the light of the visible spectrum or with other portions of the electromagnetic spectrum.
Disposable	A disposable is a product designed for cheapness and short-term convenience rather than medium to long-term durability, with most products only intended for single use. The term is also sometimes used for products that may last several months (ex. disposable air filters) to distinguish from similar products that last indefinitely (ex.
Capacity planning	Capacity planning is the process of determining the production capacity needed by an organization to meet changing demands for its products. In the context of Capacity planning, `capacity` is the maximum amount of work that an organization is capable of completing in a given period of time. The phrase is also used in business computing as a synonym for Capacity Management. A discrepancy between the capacity of an organization and the demands of its customers results in inefficiency, either in under-utilized resources or unfulfilled customers.
Gene	A Gene is the basic unit of heredity in a living organism. All living things depend on Genes. Genes hold the information to build and maintain their cells and pass Genetic traits to offspring.
Hormone	A hormone is a chemical released by one or more cells that affects cells in other parts of the organism. Only a small amount of hormone is required to alter cell metabolism. It is essentially a chemical messenger that transports a signal from one cell to another.
Communications management	Communications management is the systematic planning, implementing, monitoring, and revision of all the channels of communication within an organization, and between organizations; it also includes the organization and dissemination of new communication directives connected with an organization, network, designing internal and external communications directives, and managing the flow of information, including online communication. New technology forces constant innovation on the part of communications managers.
Contract manufacturing	Contract manufacturing is a type of manufacturing in which components or products are produced for another `hiring` firm. It is a form of outsourcing.

	The practice of utilizing Contract manufacturing relies on the manufacturer`s ability to drive down the cost of production through economies of scale.
Kidneys	The Kidneys are paired organs, which have the production of urine as their primary function. Kidneys are seen in many types of animals, including vertebrates and some invertebrates. They are an essential part of the urinary system, but have several secondary functions concerned with homeostatic functions.
Generic brands	Generic brands of consumer products (often supermarket goods) are distinguished by the absence of a brand name, although the term is actually improper usage of the word `generic`, which actually means `relating to or descriptive of an entire group or class.` Furthermore, it is often inaccurate to describe these products as `lacking a brand name`, as they usually are branded, albeit with either the brand of the store in which they are sold or a lesser-known brand name which may not be aggressively advertised to the public. They are identified more by product characteristics. They may be manufactured by less prominent companies, or manufactured on the same production line as a `named` brand.
Capital structure	In finance, Capital structure refers to the way a corporation finances its assets through some combination of equity, debt, a firm that sells $20 billion in equity and $80 billion in debt is said to be 20% equity-financed and 80% debt-financed.
Helpmates	Helpmates is a Laurel and Hardy short film comedy. It was directed by James Parrott, produced by Hal Roach and released by Metro-Goldwyn Mayer on January 23, 1932. Ollie`s house is a mess after a wild party from the previous night.
Competitive advantage	Competitive advantage is a position of a company in a competitive landscape that allows the company earning return on investments higher than the cost of investments. Competitive advantage should be relevant, unique, and sustainable. Competitive advantage is a theory that seeks to address some of the criticisms of comparative advantage.
Nominative determinism	Nominative determinism refers to the theory that a person`s name is given an influential role in reflecting key attributes of his job, profession, but real examples are more highly prized, the more obscure the better.

Market dominance	Market dominance is a measure of the strength of a brand, product, service, relative to competitive offerings. There is often a geographic element to the competitive landscape. In defining Market dominance, you must see to what extent a product, brand, or firm controls a product category in a given geographic area.
Mergers and acquisitions	The phrase Mergers and acquisitions refers to the aspect of corporate strategy, corporate finance and management dealing with the buying, selling and combining of different companies that can aid, finance, or help a growing company in a given industry grow rapidly without having to create another business entity. An acquisition, also known as a takeover or a buyout, is the buying of one company (the \`target\`) by another. Merger is when two companies combine together to form a new company alltogether.
Advanced Micro Devices	Advanced Micro Devices, Inc. is an American multinational semiconductor company based in Sunnyvale, California, that develops computer processors and related technologies for commercial and consumer markets. Its main products include microprocessors, motherboard chipsets, embedded processors and graphics processors for servers, workstations and personal computers, and processor technologies for handheld devices, digital television, automobiles, game consoles, and other embedded systems applications.
Group	In business, a group, business group, corporate group) alliance is most commonly a legal entity that is a type of conglomerate or holding company consisting of a parent company and subsidiaries. Typical examples are Adidas group or Icelandair group. In United Arab Emirates, Business group can also be knows as Trade association.
Enabling	Enabling is a term with a double meaning. As a positive term, it references patterns of interaction which allow individuals to develop and grow. These may be on any scale, for example within the family, or in wider society as \`Enabling acts\` designed to empower some group, or create a new authority for a (usually governmental) body.
Leadership	In response to the criticism of the trait approach, theorists began to research Leadership as a set of behaviors, evaluating the behavior of \`successful\` leaders, determining a behavior taxonomy and identifying broad Leadership styles. David McClelland, for example, saw Leadership skills, not so much as a set of traits, but as a pattern of motives. He claimed that successful leaders will tend to have a high need for power, a low need for affiliation, and a high level of what he called activity inhibition (one might call it self-control).

Enterprise software

Enterprise software is software that is sold to an enterprise. An enterprise here refers to an organization, such as a business or government organization. The Enterprise software is a collection of computer programs with common business applications, tools for modeling how the entire organization works, and development tools for building applications unique to the organization.

Copyright

Copyright is the set of exclusive rights granted to the author or creator of an original work, including the right to copy, distribute and adapt the work. These rights can be licensed, transferred and/or assigned. Copyright lasts for a certain time period after which the work is said to enter the public domain.

Suit

A suit is a set of garments crafted from the same cloth, consisting of at least a jacket and trousers. Lounge suits are the most common style of Western suit, originating in England as country wear. Other types of suit still worn today are firstly the dinner suit, part of black tie, which arose as a lounging alternative to dress coats in much the same way as the day lounge suit came to replace frock and morning coats; and secondly, rarely worn today, the morning suit.

Business process

A Business process or business method is a collection of related, structured activities or tasks that produce a specific service or product for a particular customer or customers. It often can be visualized with a flowchart as a sequence of activities.

Overview
There are three types of Business processes:

· Management processes, the processes that govern the operation of a system. Typical management processes include `Corporate Governance` and `Strategic Management`.

· Operational processes, processes that constitute the core business and create the primary value stream. Typical operational processes are Purchasing, Manufacturing, Marketing and Sales.

· Supporting processes, which support the core processes. Examples include Accounting, Recruitment, Technical support.

Google Maps	Google Maps is a basic web mapping service application and technology provided by Google, free (for non-commercial use), that powers many map-based services, including the Google Maps website, Google Ride Finder, Google Transit, and maps embedded on third-party websites via the Google Maps API. It offers street maps, a route planner for traveling by foot, car, or public transport and an urban business locator for numerous countries around the world. According to one of its creators (Lars Rasmussen), Google Maps is `a way of organizing the world`s information geographically`. Google Maps uses the Mercator projection, so it cannot show areas around the poles.
KMD	KMD was a hip hop trio in the early 1990s, best known for launching the career of acclaimed rapper and producer MF DOOM, who at the time was known as Zev Love X. Other members of the group were Rodan and DJ Subroc-Zev Love X`s younger brother. When Rodan chose to finish high school instead of continue working with the group Zev Love X and DJ Subroc brought in Onyx the Birthstone Kid to fill in the vacant rapping position.  After guest-starring on 3rd Bass` song `The Gas Face,` the trio released its acclaimed and overlooked full-length debut, Mr. Hood.
Supply-Chain Operations Reference	Supply-Chain Operations Reference-model is a process reference model developed by the management consulting firm PRTM and AMR Research and endorsed by the Supply-Chain Council (SCC) as the cross-industry de facto standard diagnostic tool for supply chain management. Supply Chain Operations Reference enables users to address, improve, and communicate supply chain management practices within and between all interested parties in the Extended Enterprise. Supply-Chain Operations Reference is a management tool, spanning from the supplier`s supplier to the customer`s customer.